D0423029

One-Minute Praises & Promises
from the Bible

STEVE MILLER

HARVEST HOUSE PUBLISHERS

EUGENE, OREGON

Cover by Dugan Design Group, Bloomington, Minnesota

Cover photo © Image Source Photography / Veer

ONE-MINUTE PRAISES AND PROMISES FROM THE BIBLE
Formerly *One-Minute Praises* and *One-Minite Promises*
Copyright © 2006 by Steve Miller
Published 2009 by Harvest House Publishers
Eugene, Oregon 97402
www.harvesthousepublishers.com

ISBN 978-0-7369-2098-8

Printed in China

15 16 / RDS-SK / 10 9 8 7 6 5 4

To you, the reader—
my prayer is that
the praises and promises
found in the Bible
will give you
a more exalted view of
God's glory, goodness, and grace.

Acknowledgments

With thanks to my dear wife, Becky;
to our sons Keith, Ryan,
and Nathan (and his wife Krista).

One-Minute Praises

The Benefits of Praising God 9
God's Greatness 11
God's Sovereignty 17
God's Faithfulness 27
God's Goodness 33
God's Love 41
God's Mercy 49
God's Kindness 53
God's Care 59
God's Holiness 69
God's Knowledge 73
God's Creative Power 77
God's Providence 83
God's Answers to Prayer 91
The Lord Jesus Christ 95
The Holy Spirit 107
The Bible 113
In Times of Suffering 119
In Times of Worship 129
The Hope of Heaven 137

One-Minute Promises

The Power of God's Promises 147
Love 149
Joy 155
Strength 159
Eternal Life 167
Forgiveness 173
Wisdom 181
Peace 185
Security 193
Deliverance 203
Power 213
Companionship 217
Goodness 223
Hope 229
Faithfulness 237
Sufficiency 241
Fulfillment 251
Protection 257
Comfort 261
Confidence 269
Answered Prayer 275
Success 283

Notes 288

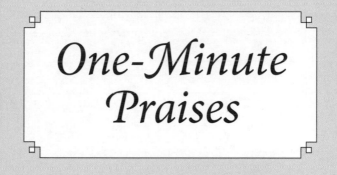

*One-Minute
Praises*

The Benefits of Praising God

From the rising of the sun to its going down
the Lord's name is to be praised.

PSALM 113:3

∽

Praise is one of the most uplifting and encouraging activities we can engage in as Christians. No prayer is complete without words of praise, and no day is complete without expressions of praise.

To praise God means to worship Him and give thanks to Him. It is to recognize who He is and what He has done, to enhance His reputation, and to express gratefulness to Him.

The psalmist wrote, "I will bless the LORD at all times; His praise shall continually be in my mouth" (Psalm 34:1). Praising God continually through the day may at first seem a challenge, but you'll discover that the more you deliberately look around you for reasons to worship and thank God, the more praise will become a habit—one that you will come to enjoy because it increases your awareness of Him, deepens your appreciation for Him, and thus draws you closer to Him.

So as you read through the one-minute praises in this book, rather than simply stop at the end of each reading, allow each page to serve as a "starter" for you—a starter that helps begin your day on a note of praise that continues throughout the day.

God's Greatness

O worship the King, all glorious above,
O gratefully sing His power and His love;
Our Shield and Defender, the Ancient of Days,
Pavilioned in splendor and girded with praise.

SIR ROBERT H. GRANT
"O WORSHIP THE KING"

Great Thoughts About a Great God

*Great is our Lord, and mighty in power;
His understanding is infinite.*

PSALM 147:5

∽

Father, how very *great* You are! You are beyond comprehension and measure. Even with all that You have revealed about Yourself in the Bible, so much about You will always be beyond my understanding.

Help me to avoid the mistake of reducing You to someone or something You are not. May I never limit You by thinking of You in human terms. My heart's desire is to lift up and honor You by always recognizing that You are "able to do exceedingly abundantly above all that we ask or think" (Ephesians 3:20).

May my every thought of You always exalt You!

A Worthy View of God

You, whose name alone is the LORD,
are the Most High over all the earth.

PSALM 83:18

∽

Nothing is above You, O Lord. You are the highest above all. You are the Supreme Ruler over all kings, kingdoms, and thrones. Everything that dwells in this universe is subject to Your authority and command.

My limited human mind cannot comprehend how infinitely great You are. And I am humbled that You, the Most High over all the heavens, have lovingly reached down to the dust of the earth to show grace, compassion, and mercy to me.

Though You have chosen to lower Yourself to walk with me, may I never lower my thoughts of You. May I never lose my sense of Your awesome majesty. May I always elevate my thoughts of You so that they are more and more worthy of You.

Incomprehensible Greatness

Great is the LORD, and greatly to be praised;
and His greatness is unsearchable.

PSALM 145:3

✑

Lord, I could never fathom the height, depth, length, and breadth of Your greatness. As I think about all that is true about You, I am moved to the depths of humility and the heights of praise.

In Your perfect wisdom, You never make a mistake. In Your perfect power, You are never defeated. In Your perfect knowledge, You are never wrong or unaware. In Your perfect faithfulness, You never break a promise. In Your perfect love, You are never unkind. In Your perfect holiness, You never sin. In Your perfect justice, You are never unfair.

I could say so much more...yet words could never suffice. I am so awed, I can only bow down before You in silent worship. Help me to be still and know that You are God.

God's Sovereignty

Even to discuss the authority of Almighty God seems
a bit meaningless, and to question it would be absurd.
Can we imagine the Lord God of Hosts
having to request permission of anyone or
to apply for anything to a higher body?
To whom would God go for permission?
Who is higher than the Highest?
Who is mightier than the Almighty?
Whose position antedates that of the Eternal?
At whose throne would God kneel?
Where is the greater one to whom He must appeal?[1]

A.W. TOZER

It's All from Him

*The earth is the LORD's, and all its fullness,
the world and those who dwell therein.*

PSALM 24:1

∽

Heavenly Father, thank You for the psalmist's affirmation that the earth is Yours—all of it. You *created* it out of nothing. You *sustain* it with a power too great for me to understand. You *govern* its ongoings according to Your perfect plans. And You *provide* for all the needs of Your creation through the resources of the land, sky, and sea.

I am richly blessed, Father, by the abundance You've placed all around me. Sometimes I don't notice it because I'm so busy or because I'm so preoccupied with the things that come from human hands rather than Your divine hands. Help me to always have a right perspective...and to begin and end every one of my days by acknowledging that ultimately, everything I have comes from You.

Achieving His Grand Purpose

Whatever the Lord pleases He does,
in heaven and in earth,
in the seas and in all deep places.

PSALM 135:6

❧

I thank You, Lord, for the Bible's many reminders of Your complete power over all things. This truth is a source of comfort for me when I see the wicked attempt to somehow thwart Your plans. I admit that sometimes I'm tempted to believe You cannot anticipate their actions, and the best You can do is minimize the damage left in their wake.

But Your Word says otherwise. No corner of the earth is so remote, no living soul so rebellious that it can act separately from Your sovereignty. You have the power to orchestrate the affairs of men, nations, and even the natural world so that they achieve Your grand purpose. Whatever You please to do *will* happen. For that I praise Your name!

Nothing Can Overrule God's Plan

Heaven and the highest heavens belong to the LORD your God, also the earth with all that is in it.

DEUTERONOMY 10:14

❦

Lord, thank You for the security and comfort that comes from knowing You are sovereign over all heaven and earth. Sometimes I get frustrated because the world seems so out of control or because I don't understand why You allow bad things to happen. Help me to not despair over what I don't understand, but instead, to trust in what the Bible says about You—that the earth and heavens belong to You.

Because of this truth, I can have full confidence that everything You plan *will* come to pass. That You *will* prevail over those who oppose You and Your children. That You *will* wipe away all sin and sorrow. And that You *will* set up Your perfect and glorious kingdom, which *will* last forever and ever.

A Sovereignty We Can Trust

Yours, O LORD, is the greatness,
the power and the glory,
the victory and the majesty;
for all that is in heaven and earth is Yours…
and You are exalted as head over all.

1 CHRONICLES 29:11

∽

Heavenly Father, Your sovereignty has no limits. Words are not adequate to describe the extent of Your rule over the universe. Your throne had no beginning and will have no end. You are all-powerful over all things at all times. No greatness is higher than Yours.

Because You are in full control of all that is in heaven and earth, I can rest assured You are also in full control of every detail of my life. Nothing will happen to me without Your permission. Though I may not understand why some things come my way, I can trust that You have a purpose and that no person will overrule You. How comforting it is to know I will never be exposed to anything that is beyond Your control! Yours is a sovereignty I can trust.

More than Adequate

*I know that You can do everything,
and that no purpose of Yours
can be withheld from You.*

JOB 42:2

∽

Lord, my human perspective is so limited. Just because something looks impossible to me doesn't mean it's impossible to You. Just because I cannot see the answer doesn't mean You lack one.

You are sovereign, so I know You are supreme over every circumstance in my life regardless of how severe it is. Your good purpose will always win out. You will never be defeated...and consequently, neither will I. Help me to not become distraught by temporary tribulation but to be calmed by Your permanent providence.

Thank You, Father, that I can rest on the bedrock of Your sovereignty even in the harshest of life's storms. Your power is far more than adequate to handle my every need!

Supreme over All

In Your hand is there not power and might,
so that no one is able to withstand You?

2 CHRONICLES 20:6

❦

Lord of all, every single one of Your decrees have been or will be fulfilled. Every person and every creature on this earth—willingly or unwillingly—is as wet clay on Your potter's wheel. You are able to use even the plots of Your enemies to accomplish whatever You please.

I praise You that Your power is so great none can defy it, Your throne is so high none can overthrow it, and Your counsel is so established none can change it.

That You are supreme over all gives me great security—for it means nothing can happen to me apart from Your plans, nothing can deprive me of Your promises, and nothing can interrupt Your provision from flowing to me.

Lord of the Possible

Oh, give thanks to the LORD! Call upon His name;
make known His deeds among the peoples!

PSALM 105:1

✑

Lord, from a human perspective, it should have been impossible to create something out of nothing. For the whole earth to be covered by a flood. For the Red Sea to part and close up again. For mere shouts and trumpets to fell the walls of Jericho. For Gideon's 300 to defeat an enemy of thousands upon thousands. For Daniel to survive a lions' den, and for his friends to walk unscathed in a fiery furnace. For a virgin to give birth. For the Lord Jesus to heal multitudes, walk on water, and rise from the dead to forever conquer death. And for me who was dead in sin to become alive in Christ.

Yet You have accomplished every one of these mighty deeds...and more. Whenever I doubt You, Lord, remind me of Your great works. You are the Lord of the possible!

God's Faithfulness

Far above all finite comprehension
is the unchanging faithfulness of God.
Everything about God is great, vast,
incomparable. He never forgets, never fails,
never falters, never forfeits His word.[2]

A.W. PINK

Always Faithful

Has God forgotten to be gracious?
Has He in anger shut up His tender mercies?…
I will remember the works of the LORD;
surely I will remember Your wonders of old.

PSALM 77:9-11

၈

Father, sometimes I struggle and wonder if You've forgotten me. When I consider my circumstances, I see problems that remain unsolved. I feel as if, for some reason, You aren't at work in my life. I've even doubted Your love and care.

Yet I know Your track record of faithfulness. When I look back, I can remember those so very clear times You rescued me. Those times when You gave me a blessing greater than I ever expected. Those times when You answered my prayers in the most powerful way.

When life isn't going so well, help me to remember Your mighty deeds and wonders of old. They're written all over the Bible, and they're written on the tablet of my life. And may the confidence I receive from what You've done in the past give me renewed courage for the future.

He Is Able

There is nothing too hard for You.

JEREMIAH 32:17

∽

Heavenly Father, Your faithfulness and sovereignty amaze me.

Whatever You start, You finish. Whatever You promise, You fulfill. No problem is too great for You to handle; no circumstance is beyond Your control.

The knowledge that nothing can derail Your plans and promises for me is a source of great comfort—especially as I struggle against my human weaknesses and failings. As Philippians 1:6 says, I can be confident that the work You began in me *will* be carried on to completion. I praise You that one day, my struggles will be no more. I will have a glorified body and dwell with You in heaven forever and ever…all because You are faithful.

Every Promise Kept

There has not failed one word of all His good promise.

1 Kings 8:56

❧

Father, I praise You that Your promises never fail. You always keep Your word, as the pages of Scripture make clear. The evidence of Your faithfulness is overwhelming.

And yet when I consider Your promises to me, I admit sometimes I become anxious. When You don't seem to be meeting my needs or answering my prayers, I get impatient, wondering when You're going to come to my rescue.

Help me to remember that in the Bible, some promises weren't fulfilled for months, years, and even centuries. Yet You have always fulfilled Your perfect plan in Your perfect time. I praise You for teaching me to wait...so that my confidence in You may grow stronger than ever.

Forever the Same

I am the LORD, I do not change....

MALACHI 3:6

❧

You are always faithful, even when I go astray. You are always wise, even when I question You. You are always in control, even when I defy Your will.

You are always attentive, even when I'm not listening. You are always just, even when I feel You're unfair. You are always seeking my best, even when I'm at my worst.

I praise You for always loving me, even when I am uncaring. I praise You for always pursuing me, even when I am unworthy. And I praise You for always being You, regardless of what I do.

God's Goodness

God only is infinitely good. A boundless goodness
that knows no limits, a goodness as infinite as his essence,
not only good, but best; not only good, but goodness itself,
the supreme inconceivable goodness.[3]

STEPHEN CHARNOCK

An Enduring Goodness

The LORD is good;
His mercy is everlasting,
and His truth endures to all generations.

PSALM 100:5

❧

Thank You, Lord, for the Bible's many assurances of Your goodness. In the times when I am tempted to question You, may I remember that Your goodness is absolutely perfect in every way. It is a goodness that does not make mistakes, and it is a goodness that emanates from every part of Your nature. It's who You are!

And I praise You that Your mercies are everlasting. They will never run dry; they will never be revoked. The mercies You poured out on the great men and women of the Bible are the same mercies I can count on today...and tomorrow and forever.

Your goodness and mercies, O Lord, fill me with a warm sense of security. Yes, great is Your faithfulness!

God Is Good

Give thanks to the LORD, for He is good!
For His mercy endures forever.

PSALM 107:1

ॐ

Lord, Your Word says repeatedly that You are good. I know that's true because of the evidence I've seen in my life. And yet sometimes the dark clouds of tragedy or pain hinder my ability to see Your goodness.

What about horrible disasters that take many lives? What about terrible injustices in which people are grievously wronged? And what about the losses, hurts, and disappointments in my own life that don't seem to make sense?

At times like these, I need to remember that You are God, and I'm not. The hard questions of life are not mine to answer but Yours. I praise You that regardless of what happens, I can know with certainty that You *are* good.

His Many Benefits

Taste and see that the LORD *is good....*

PSALM 34:8

✍

How great, O Father, is Your goodness! I cannot comprehend its immensity. Nor do I always recognize it for what it is. Yet may I always acknowledge Your favor and kindness upon me. May I always praise You for every benefit You have given me, regardless of how small.

Because of Your goodness, You continue to give me life and breath. You continue to bless me with spiritual riches and eternal hope. You continue to provide for my every need and preserve me in my every circumstance.

Where, O Lord, would I be without Your favor? Your Word says that every good thing I have in life is from You (James 1:17). May my heart treasure every good gift You have given to me, and may everything I do today magnify Your goodness.

His Goodness Is Unchanging

Oh, give thanks to the LORD, for He is good!

PSALM 106:1

∽

Your goodness, dear Lord, is the fountain from which all blessings flow. It is spontaneous and generous; it is perfect and eternal. It cannot be earned; neither can it be repaid. So abundant is Your goodness that You make the sun to shine on the unrighteous as well as the righteous and send the rain to pour on the unjust as well as the just. Your goodness is evident in everything You do, from the outpouring of Your love to the exercising of Your justice.

When I am tempted to doubt Your goodness, remind me that it is unchanging. Teach me to look for Your goodness even when I am overwhelmed by sorrow and tribulation. And help me to rest in Your faithfulness, which assures me that Your goodness will always endure.

The Magnitude of His Blessings

Blessed be the Lord,
who daily loads us with benefits,
the God of our salvation!

PSALM 68:19

❦

Lord, who am I that You have favored me so greatly? You have made me in Your image, given me the breath of life, and made possible my salvation so that I may enjoy a personal relationship with You.

You have surrounded me with the majestic splendor of the heavens and the earth. Every day, I see and experience new testimonies to Your creativity, power, and wisdom. You have filled the world with good things for my pleasure and my provision.

I am filled with admiration at the magnitude of Your goodness to me. With each new morning, may I look around me afresh and determine to fully savor every blessing I receive from Your hand. May I never fail to praise You for all You've given to me.

God's Love

As Christians…we ought to see that everything we enjoy in life—from our tiniest pleasures to the eternal redemption we have found in Christ—is an expression of the great love wherewith God loved us. The blessing of His love comes to us not because we deserve it, but simply and only because of His sovereign grace.…In light of the glories of divine love, how can we not be utterly lost in wonder, love, and praise?[4]

JOHN MACARTHUR

An Inexhaustible Love

I will cry out to God Most High,
to God who performs all things for me.

PSALM 57:2

∽

I am both awed and humbled, Lord, when I consider that You are God Most High, and yet You involve Yourself so intimately in my life. You are never too busy for me, and none of my concerns are too insignificant for You.

You are my Rock, my Fortress, my Shepherd. You are my Friend, my Champion, my Deliverer. You delight in me as Your child, lavish Your love on me, and guide me through every circumstance. Though You are ruler over all the universe, Your care for me is so complete it's as if nothing else existed. Yes, You are a God "who performs all things for me."

Thank You that I cannot exhaust all the ways You express Your care. How precious to me is Your love!

His Perfect Love for Us

*Behold what manner of love the Father has
bestowed on us, that we should be called
children of God!*

1 John 3:1

∽

Lord, I praise You that Your love for me has no limits.
It's a love that cares for me in spite of all my shortcomings.
You love me because You *want* to, not because You *have* to.
And You are faithful to show Your love to me even when
I'm not faithful to You.

Your love is a perfect love—it is…

a love that is consistent,
a love that is constant,
a love that is complete.

Your perfect love knows exactly what I need and when
I need it…whether it be encouragement, guidance, or
even correction. And it is a love that has chosen to make
me Your child. How generous, how magnificent, how
indescribable is Your love!

A Many-Splendored Love

You, O Lord, are a God full of compassion, and gracious,
longsuffering and abundant in mercy and truth.

PSALM 86:15

∾

Heavenly Father, Your love for me is manifest in so many ways!

Your compassion comforts me in the midst of my hurts and weaknesses. Your grace redeems me from condemnation and showers me with blessings though I do not deserve them. Your longsuffering is a divine patience that never gives up on me when I question or fail You. Your mercy chooses to forgive my sin and make me a citizen of heaven. And Your truth guides me and gives me wisdom and hope for all the days of my life.

I am lost in wonder when I consider the immensity of Your love for me. It will stand forever and never cease to be. May I bring more praise to You by letting Your many-splendored love shine through my life to others.

A Love Without Parallel

God demonstrates His own love toward us, in that
while we were still sinners, Christ died for us.

ROMANS 5:8

∽

Father, of all the praises I could ever sing to You, surely the greatest by far is praise for what Your Son did on the cross. There the world can see the most glorious display of divine love human eyes have ever witnessed. Yours is a love without parallel, a love undeserved, a love stronger than death.

How brightly did Your love shine as Jesus bled on the cross—as He endured the brutal nails, the piercing thorns, the excruciating pain! I should have paid the price, and yet Your Son graciously took my place and endured the fullness of Your wrath.

I am humbled, Lord, by the greatness of Your love for me. May every single day of my life be filled to overflowing with gratitude and adoration for You.

Infinite Love

*In this is love, not that we loved God, but that He
loved us and sent His Son....*

1 JOHN 4:10

∽

Father, it was Jesus' infinite love that led Him to kneel
in agony and pray, "Not as I will, but as You will." It was
His infinite love that led Him to endure betrayal, arrest,
and injustice. It was His infinite love that enabled Him
to bear the cruel scourging and the indescribable horrors
of the crucifixion.

Because He took on my sin, I can one day be holy.
Because He was willing to die on the cross, I can one day
live in Your kingdom. And because He wore a crown of
thorns, I can one day wear a crown of glory.

Thank You, Father, for all that Your Son's love has
accomplished. It is a love too great to fathom, a love for
which I could never give enough thanks. May His infinite
love for me inspire infinite praise from me!

God's Mercy

When all Thy mercies, O my God,
My rising soul surveys,
Transported with the view, I'm lost
In wonder, love and praise.
Unnumbered comforts to my soul
Thy tender care bestowed
Before my infant heart conceived
From whom those comforts flowed.

JOSEPH ADDISON
"WHEN ALL THY MERCIES, O MY GOD"

Rejoicing in His Mercy

For as the heavens are high above the earth,
so great is His mercy toward those who fear Him.

PSALM 103:11

~

Father, I praise You for Your incredible mercy. As I look back on the times I have failed You, I realize You have given me second chances, third chances, and more. When I have stumbled and succumbed to temptation, You have stood nearby, ready to pick me up. When I have asked forgiveness for my trespasses, You have lavished it upon me freely.

I am humbled when I consider the extent of Your mercy. It burst forth as a fountain when You chose to save me in eternity past and will flow as a steady stream all the way into eternity future. Your mercy is new every morning and blesses me all the day long. Because of Your mercy, Lord, I have confidence for today and hope for tomorrow!

Abundant in Mercy

You, Lord, are good, and ready to forgive,
and abundant in mercy to all those who call upon You.

PSALM 86:5

∽

My heart rejoices over Your goodness to me, Lord. When I confess my sin, You are ready to forgive. Your mercies are constant, and Your compassions are new every morning.

Though at times I slip and fall, You are patient with me. With tenderness You pick me up and restore me. With lovingkindness You come alongside me and instruct me in the ways of righteousness.

Lord, I long for my life to be pleasing to You. And I praise You that I am not left to do this in my own power. You have been generous beyond what I could ever expect, and You have given me every resource I need. Thank You for Your incredible mercy!

God's Kindness

O God, I cannot number, I cannot express by words,
all the instances of thy fatherly kindness.
But so long as I live I will boast of thy grace,
and prolong in eternity that thanksgiving
which I have here so imperfectly begun.[5]

CHRISTOPHER CHRISTIAN STURM

Remembering His Kindness

I will mention the lovingkindnesses of the LORD and the praises of the LORD, according to all that the LORD has bestowed on us.

ISAIAH 63:7

∽

Father, help me not forget the many ways You've shown Your love for me. Your kindness to me began even before the foundation of the world, when You chose me to receive the gifts of salvation and eternal life. And Your goodness continues to be manifest in the ways You provide for all my physical and spiritual needs.

When I preoccupy myself with anxieties about the future, I easily lose sight of Your kindness in the past. Refresh my mind and heart with reminders of Your faithfulness. May the many lights of Your past kindnesses shine their rays forward and melt away the darkness and uncertainty that cover the path before me.

Above all, may my lips proclaim and praise Your kind acts so that others, too, may see how great You are.

Secure in His Kindness

The mountains shall depart and the hills be removed,
but My kindness shall not depart from you....

∾

Father, You care for me as no one else can. You know my needs better than I do. While I cannot see past today's crises and circumstances, You can see all my tomorrows, and You are able to bring about the ultimate good that I have yet to understand.

I admit that when I'm faced with troubles and uncertainty, resting completely in Your loving and sovereign hands is hard for me. In my mind I know You are faithful, but in my heart I still struggle with fear.

Thank You for the promise that Your kindness will never depart from me. Because You are in control and You care, I have no reason to be afraid. May I always rest secure in You!

A Fount of Blessing

*What shall I render to the LORD
for all His benefits toward me?*

PSALM 116:12

∽

I love You, Lord, for giving me another day in which to experience Your kindness and grace. Every new morning is another gift from You, another opportunity to watch for the many mercies You send my way.

I can easily lose sight of the evidences of Your kindness in my life. Help me to watch for even the tiniest of blessings…in my family and friendships, in my work, in my home, in my church, and even in my meals and rest and play. And as I recognize Your gifts to me, may I immediately lift up praise to You, knowing that every good thing comes from Your hand.

You hold power over all my life; may I never take a single day or a single act of Your kindness for granted. What a fount of blessing You are to me!

Chosen for His Work

*To each one is given the manifestation of the
Spirit for the common good.*

1 CORINTHIANS 12:7 NASB

༄

Lord, Your kindness and generosity never cease to amaze me. Not only have You saved me and are You changing me, but You have also gifted me to fulfill a needed role in Your church. With perfect foresight, You knew exactly where I could be of greatest use…for the good of others in the body of Christ.

I thank You that no Christian is a mere spectator and that all are participants. You've placed me among fellow believers who can minister to me as I minister to them. I marvel at how You have interwoven all our lives so that when we work together, individual needs are met and the whole church is built up.

I know You don't need me to help do Your work on earth, Lord…yet You've chosen to work through me. What a gracious God You are!

God's Care

Come, Thou Fount of every blessing,
Tune my heart to sing Thy grace;
Streams of mercy, never ceasing,
Call for songs of loudest praise.
Teach me some melodious sonnet,
Sung by flaming tongues above;
Praise His name! I'm fixed upon it!
Name of God's redeeming love.

ROBERT ROBINSON
"COME, THOU FOUNT"

Always Watching

*The eyes of the LORD are on the righteous,
and His ears are open to their cry.*

PSALM 34:15

∽

Father, You watch over me every day and every night without ceasing. All Your thoughts about me are thoughts of fatherly love and concern.

Your eyes are so attentively focused on me, I know I have no reason to fear my safety. Your arms are protectively folded around me as if I were Your one and only child. Your ears are so alert to my cries for help, I know You will always intercede in times of trouble.

Because of Your watchfulness, I have no reason to be anxious. To fret and worry would be to doubt and dishonor You. All through the ages You have never failed to care for any of Your own, and I know You will never fail to care for me. Thank You that I can always count on Your faithfulness!

A Solid Rock

*He...set my feet upon a rock,
and established my steps.*

PSALM 40:2

∽

Lord, if I can always count on anyone or anything, it's You and Your care. People will let me down, but You won't. Circumstances will cause me to slip and fall, but You are faithful to pick me up and place me where I can stand firm.

Remind me to always place my confidence not in myself but in You. You alone are the solid ground, the firm foundation upon which I need to place my life. And You alone are able to lift me up and establish me on the sure and everlasting rock of Your protection and peace.

Should I ever begin to place confidence in myself, help me to recognize it and relinquish it to You. Whatever happens in my life, Lord, I want it to be the result of Your divine accomplishment and not my human achievement.

A Guide We Can Trust

Trust in the LORD with all your heart,
and lean not on your own understanding;
in all your ways acknowledge Him,
and He shall direct your paths.

PROVERBS 3:5-6

∾

Thank You, Lord, that I don't have to figure out everything on my own. Sometimes life feels so out of control, and I'm not sure what I should do next. All around me, I hear the message that I need to be self-sufficient. But I know that doesn't really work— and that when I fail to consult You, I tend to mess things up.

Thank You that I can turn to You for guidance at any time. You are more than delighted to teach me, enlighten me, and lead me in the way I should go. You promise that if I place my full trust in You, You *will* direct my path.

Help me to rest in You and let You manage my life. I know that when I do, I won't feel so stressed or anxious.

All This and More

I will call upon the LORD, who is worthy to be praised.

2 SAMUEL 22:4

∞

Heavenly Father, whenever doubt creeps into my heart and I begin to question Your care for me, help me to remember...

Regardless of the temptations I face, You have provided a way of escape. Even when my sin is great, Your love and forgiveness are greater. As much as I may waver, Your faithfulness is firm as ever. Regardless of how destitute I may feel, You will always provide for me. As high as the mountain before me may rise, You are higher still. Regardless of what attempts to hinder my relationship with You, nothing can separate me from Your love.

In every way, Father, You are higher...deeper...and greater. In every way You will sustain me, and You are worthy of unceasing praise!

Trusting, Leaning, and Praising

Hear my cry, O God; attend to my prayer....
When my heart is overwhelmed;
lead me to the rock that is higher than I.

PSALM 61:1-2

∽

Father, help me to recognize that true happiness comes only when I surrender all my concerns to You. Help me to remember that true relief comes only when I place all my burdens in Your hands. Teach me, O Lord, when sorrows surround me, not to seek their removal but to let Your will be done.

This is my heart's desire, Lord, because I want to lean not on my own might but Yours. Not on my own wisdom but Yours. And not on my own plans but Yours.

Lord, I want You to be my everything. I realize that until You are my all, I actually have nothing. Help me to trust You more, lean on You more, and above all, praise You more.

Always Alert

He who keeps you will not slumber.

PSALM 121:3

∾

Lord, You are my Keeper, my Protector, my Shepherd. Your watchfulness over me is constant and will never cease. You never grow tired; Your eyes never close. Though You rule over all the universe, the magnitude of Your work never fatigues You.

Because You are always alert, I have nothing to fear. No intruder—whether an enemy or a temptation—will ever catch You by surprise. Though the path of life may be dangerous and difficult at times, You will preserve me. As the psalmist said, "Even though I walk through the valley of the shadow of death, I will fear no evil, for you are with me" (Psalm 23:4 NIV).

Because You are always alert, I am able to rest. I am able to lie down in green pastures and beside still waters. Thank You, Lord, for the security Your attentive care gives to me.

A Patient Father

Gracious is the LORD, and righteous;
yes, our God is merciful.

PSALM 116:5

༄

Father, I sometimes don't learn very well, do I? I wouldn't be surprised if You're frustrated with me. I've fallen into this temptation before. And the blame is all mine. You promised a way of escape, and I didn't take it.

I thank You that You will never give up on me. How gentle Your longsuffering, how tender Your patience. Though I plunge into sin, You reach out to lift me up. In Your kindness, You are willing to restore me. Shouldn't I have learned this lesson already?

I marvel at Your patience, Father. May I never abuse it through deliberate disobedience. Convict me, and may I cry out to You for the strength and the will to choose the way of holiness.

God's Holiness

Holy, Holy, Holy! Though the darkness hide Thee,
Though the eye of sinful man Thy glory may not see,
Only Thou art Holy; there is none beside Thee
Perfect in power, in love, and purity.

REGINALD HEBER
"HOLY, HOLY, HOLY"

An Absolute Holiness

*Exalt the LORD our God,
and worship at His holy hill;
for the LORD our God is holy.*

PSALM 99:9

∽

Father, Your holiness is too great for me to fathom. It is so perfect, so pure, so unapproachable. It is so all-encompassing that all Your attributes are holy. Your wisdom is holy, Your love is holy, Your justice is holy, Your power is holy...everything about You is holy and therefore is worthy of praise!

In light of Your absolute holiness, I realize You cannot allow sin in Your presence. Illuminate my mind and direct my will so that I may resist temptation. Prompt me to flee from anything that would hinder my fellowship with You and soil my service to You. May my fear of Your holiness come from a reverence that desires to please You and a love that is determined not to grieve You. Remind me that when I am holy, I bring honor and glory to You.

The Benefits of His Holiness

Holy, holy, holy is the LORD of hosts;
The whole earth is full of His glory!

ISAIAH 6:3

∾

Lord, how beautiful is Your holiness! Every word You say and every work You do is perfect, pure, and undefiled. Every one of Your laws and judgments is altogether righteous. No trace of wrong or evil is in You.

Help me to never take Your holiness for granted. Without it, the cross and my salvation would have been impossible. I would be forever imprisoned in the dungeon of sin and darkness. Because of Your holiness, I am now free to enjoy the light of Your glory and grace.

And because You are holy, I know You will always deal with me truthfully, rightly, and fairly. Though I cannot always trust people, I know I can always trust You. I praise and thank You for what Your holiness means to me.

God's Knowledge

God perfectly knows Himself and,
being the source and author of all things,
it follows that He knows all that can be known.
And this He knows instantly and with a fullness
of perfection that includes every possible item
of knowledge concerning everything that exists
or could have existed anywhere in the universe
at any time in the past or that may exist
in the centuries or ages yet unborn.[6]

A.W. TOZER

Resting in His Perfect Knowledge

Oh, the depth of the riches both of the wisdom and knowledge of God! How unsearchable are His judgments and His ways past finding out!

ROMANS 11:33

❧

Father, You know everything. Nothing is hidden from You, and You have a perfect knowledge of the future.

This gives me *security,* because I know nothing will ever happen that takes You by surprise.

This gives me *peace,* because I know I can always turn to You when I don't have the answers.

This gives me *confidence,* because I know whatever You say will happen really *will* happen.

This gives me *comfort,* because I know You can see all my tomorrows, and You will lead me through them.

Thank You, Father, that Your perfect knowledge of all things can serve, for me, as a source of perfect peace in all things.

He Knows Us Well

You know my sitting down and my rising up;
You understand my thought afar off.
You comprehend my path and my lying down,
and are acquainted with all my ways.

PSALM 139:2-3

∾

Dear Lord, nothing in my life escapes Your notice, and You never forget anything. You have known me from before time began, and You know me better than I know myself.

Because You know everything perfectly, You know my every need and are able to take perfect care of me. You understand my every frailty and are able to provide perfect help for me. You know my every thought and are able to provide perfect counsel to me—whether it be conviction, direction, or encouragement.

That You know me so well gives me great comfort, Lord. That Your knowledge is perfect makes You a perfect Father and Friend for me.

God's Creative Power

All Thy works with joy surround Thee,
Earth and heaven reflect Thy rays,
Stars and angels sing around Thee,
Center of unbroken praise;
Field and forest, vale and mountain,
Flowering meadow, flashing sea,
Chanting bird and flowing fountain,
Call us to rejoice in Thee.

HENRY J. VAN DYKE
"JOYFUL, JOYFUL, WE ADORE THEE"

A Testimony of His Power

The heavens declare the glory of God;
and the firmament shows His handiwork.

PSALM 19:1

❧

Day and night, Father, I am reminded of how great You are. Every one of the heavenly bodies—the sun by day, and the planets and stars by night—moves with astounding mathematical precision and reliability. Their perfect order is a silent yet profound testimony of Your complete power over all the universe.

I praise You that Your greatness is so clearly manifest all around me, for it wonderfully reminds me, at all times, of what You can do. May the beauty and order of the heavens inspire within me a deeper trust and confidence in You—a confidence that realizes that if You are in full control of the universe, surely You are in full control of my life.

How Marvelous His Works!

You formed my inward parts;
You covered me in my mother's womb.
I will praise You, for I am
fearfully and wonderfully made....

PSALM 139:13-14

&

Father, when I think about the incredible complexity and design of the human body, I never cease to be amazed. And the more that science learns, the more we realize how little we really know. Our bodies are awesome testimonies of the infinite greatness of Your wisdom and creativity.

I am especially in awe of the way my body sustains itself. My heartbeat, my breathing, and so many other processes continue to carry on without any effort on my part. Billions of cells are at work in a marvelous harmony that keeps me functioning...even when I am asleep!

I magnify You, Lord, for I am fearfully and wonderfully made. May I always honor Your handiwork by taking good care of what You've given me.

God's Greatness on Display

Praise Him, sun and moon;
praise Him, all you stars of light!
Praise Him, you heavens of heavens,
and you waters above the heavens!
Let them praise the name of the LORD,
for He commanded and they were created.

PSALM 148:3-5

෴

Lord, Your name is written on all Your works. Everything You created shouts with loudest praises what a wonderful God You are.

As I look at the immensity of Your creation, I see Your greatness. As I consider the complexity of Your works, I see Your wisdom. As I admire their beauty and usefulness, I realize Your goodness. And when I am reminded that You made them all from nothing, I am awed by Your power.

I am especially amazed when I remember that Your greatness, wisdom, goodness, and power have no beginning and no end. May I proclaim Your majesty with the same enthusiasm as all nature does!

The Crowning Glory of Creation

All Your works shall praise You, O Lord,
and Your saints shall bless You.

Psalm 145:10

✍

God of wonders, every part of Your creation magnifies Your greatness. Every creature in the earth, sea, and sky displays the beauty of Your handiwork. Every mountain, ocean, planet, and star proclaims the enormity of Your power. And yet when You created man and woman, You went above and beyond—You made them in Your very own image.

I am filled with awe that You chose to make humankind the crowning glory of Your creation. You gave us a special worth; we alone can know You in a personal and meaningful way. And even when we fell into sin, You chose to send a Redeemer and save us…showing how so very much You love us.

You alone, O Lord, are worthy of all praise!

God's Providence

Praise to the Lord, who o'er all things so wondrously reigneth,
Shelters thee under His wings, yea, so gently sustaineth!
Hast thou not seen How thy desires e'er have been
Granted in what He ordaineth!

JOACHIM NEANDER
"PRAISE TO THE LORD, THE ALMIGHTY"

The Source of True Riches

*Blessed be the God and Father of our Lord Jesus
Christ, who according to His abundant mercy has
begotten us…to an inheritance incorruptible and
undefiled and that does not fade away, reserved in
heaven for you.…*

1 PETER 1:3-4

❧

Lord, how I wish I were not so easily seduced by
the glittering attractions of this world. All too often I am
drawn to the empty treasures of this earth rather than
the satisfying riches of Your grace. You have given to me
the everlasting wealth of spiritual life and Your future
kingdom…and yet still I pursue contentment from that
which will one day turn to dust.

Oh, that I would take greater delight in hiding Your
Word in my heart, communing with You all day long,
and appreciating Your blessings in my life. May I seek
fulfillment in loving, serving, and praising You. Help me
to let go of the insignificant so that my hands and heart
are free to cling instead to that which is significant.

I praise You, Lord, for all the riches I possess in
You.

All Things Are Possible

I can do all things through Christ who strengthens me.

PHILIPPIANS 4:13

❧

Lord Jesus, I thank You that You don't expect me to live the Christian life in my own power. I admit that in my human weakness, obeying Your more difficult commands is hard. You say, "Love your enemies...do good to those who hate you, and pray for those who...persecute you" (Matthew 5:44). Lord, that's *very* hard to do!

Yet You also say, "Abide in me" so that You may enable me (John 15:4). You say, "Walk in the Spirit" so that I may bear the Spirit's fruit (Galatians 5:16,22-23). And You say to let Your Word dwell in me richly so that it may transform me (Colossians 3:16).

Yes, I *can* do all things because of the resources You've given me. All You ask is that I be an open and willing vessel. Thank You for Your provision!

We Have Everything

His divine power has given to us all things that
pertain to life and godliness.

2 PETER 1:3

∽

Father, You have given me *everything* I need for life
and godliness. You have given me...

Your Son Jesus, who made my salvation possible. He is
also the vine that enables me, the branch, to bear fruit. As
the apostle Paul said, I am *complete* in Christ (Colossians
2:10).

Your Holy Spirit, who is my Counselor and Comforter.
Thank You for the promise that the Spirit will guide me
in *all* truth (John 16:13).

And Your Word, which guides and corrects me so that
I "may be thoroughly equipped for *every* good work"
(2 Timothy 3:16-17 NIV).

In You, Father, I lack nothing. Thank You for giving
so abundantly to me!

His Perfect Timing

Though the LORD is on high,
yet He regards the lowly....

PSALM 138:6

✍

Lord, I am awed as I consider that You stand above time. You can see all of eternity past and eternity future simultaneously. Time does not hem You in; rather, You are its master. You coordinate everything that happens on this earth according to Your perfect will. Nothing ever takes place too early or too late.

As I journey through the Bible, I see again and again how You cared for Your people in their moments of need, always at the right time. May that bring confidence to my heart whenever I become anxious about the future. Help me to rest and wait for Your provision…which I know will come at the perfect time. I have no need to worry about tomorrow, for You are already there.

Thank You, Lord

In everything give thanks....
1 THESSALONIANS 5:18

✍

Father, help me to realize the power of having a thankful heart. When I am grateful for what I have, Satan cannot sow the seeds of discontent in me.

When I am dissatisfied with my place in life, remind me to be grateful that I am even alive. When I complain about my responsibilities, stir me to gratitude that I was entrusted with them. When I resent others needing my help, cause me to be thankful that I can bring blessing into their lives.

May my every negative attitude, Lord, become positive through thankfulness to You. Teach me to truly give thanks in *everything*, for I know gratitude makes the difference between discouragement and joy.

God's Answers to Prayer

*O Lord, in looking back we are obliged to remember
with the greatest gratitude the many occasions
in which Thou hast heard our cry.
We have been brought into deep distress,
and our heart has sunk within us,
and then have we cried to Thee and
Thou has never refused to hear us.*[7]

CHARLES HADDON SPURGEON

He Hears Our Every Cry

Give ear to my words, O LORD,
consider my meditation.
Give heed to the voice of my cry,
my King and my God,
for to You I will pray.

PSALM 5:1-2

❧

Lord, thank You that You are always ready to hear my voice. Thank You for the psalmist's affirmation that I really am important to You. I don't need to beg You to hear me, for You *promise* to hear me!

And You hear not only my prayers but also those cries and anxieties that I cannot express. The assurance that You hear and understand me at all times brings great comfort and calm to my heart.

And Father, when I pray, may I be as willing to hear Your voice as You are to hear mine. May I listen to Your words to me in the Scriptures. May I seek, at all times, to accept the way You answer my prayers.

He Will Answer

In the day of my trouble I will call upon You,
for You will answer me.

PSALM 86:7

∽

Heavenly Father, when I am tossed to and fro by life's difficulties, I tend to allow fear and doubt to fill my mind. But when the storms pass and the sunshine returns, I look back in hindsight and can see clear evidence of Your guiding hand upon my life.

I see Your *incredible wisdom* in the way You allowed me to grow through the experience. I see Your *unceasing compassion* in the way You preserved me and brought help. I see Your *unfailing love* in the good that came out of the bad.

When I cry out to You, O Lord, I know You will answer. Your response may not be immediate, but I know it will come. I praise You for Your faithfulness to me in the past, and I know Your faithfulness to me will continue into the future.

The Lord Jesus Christ

All hail the power of Jesus' name!
Let angels prostrate fall;
Bring forth the royal diadem
And crown Him Lord of all!
Bring forth the royal diadem
And crown Him Lord of all!

Let every kindred, every tribe,
On this terrestrial ball,
To Him all majesty ascribe,
And crown Him Lord of all!
To Him all majesty ascribe,
And crown Him Lord of all!

EDWARD PERRONET
"ALL HAIL THE POWER OF JESUS' NAME"

With a Grateful Heart

Thanks be to God for His indescribable gift!

2 Corinthians 9:15

∞

Father, *nothing* is more wonderful than what Jesus did for me at the cross. As the song proclaims, "Amazing love! How can it be that Thou my God shouldst die for me?"

I marvel as I consider the high price You paid so I could become Your child. You could have given up on me as hopelessly lost, but You didn't. Out of Your great love, for reasons I cannot explain, You chose to rescue me from the inescapable shackles of sin.

The suffering that Jesus endured on my behalf causes me to bow my head in quiet gratitude. I lift up my heart to You in worship…and may I *always* be filled with wonder because of the magnitude of Your love and grace!

The Beauty of His Humility

Jesus, who, being in the form of God…made Himself of no reputation, taking the form of a bondservant….

PHILIPPIANS 2:5-6

❧

Jesus, though You are King of kings and Lord of lords and You are worthy of the highest honor and praise, You did not cling to Your position and Your glory when the time came to redeem humanity.

You did not consider Yourself too great to become a bondservant and grow up in poverty. You were not too proud to touch the untouchables and love the unlovable. You were not too significant to teach uneducated fishermen and ride on a donkey. No person was unimportant to You, no child was too small for You, no task was too menial. The sacrifices You made in Your life were many—even to the point of death!

Lord, You humbled Yourself that I might be exalted. May Your humility inspire me…and may I never consider myself too great to do the little things You have called me to do.

What a Savior!

In Christ Jesus you who once were far off
have been brought near by the blood of Christ.

EPHESIANS 2:13

∽

Jesus, I bow before You in silent adoration as I consider what You have done for me. You have rescued me from death. Cleansed me of sin. Lifted me from shame. Freed me from guilt. Raised me to life. Filled me with hope. Clothed me with righteousness. Calmed me with peace. Upheld me with strength. And secured me for heaven.

How can I express my gratitude to You? By glorying in Your cross. Resting in Your grace. Following in Your steps. Listening to Your words. Trusting in Your provision. Relying on Your faithfulness. Marveling in Your love. And rejoicing in Your promise of eternity with You.

Praising Christ for All Eternity

Worthy is the Lamb who was slain
to receive power and riches and wisdom,
and strength and honor and glory and blessing!

REVELATION 5:12

∽

Yes, Jesus, You are worthy of honor and glory! My every hope, my every blessing in life is possible because of You alone. Without Your sacrifice on the cross, I would have nothing. Because of Your precious blood shed at Calvary, I have everything.

Whatever praises come my way, may I pass them along to You. Whatever benefits I enjoy in life, remind me to thank You. Whatever rewards and crowns I gain here on earth, may I cast them at Your feet in heaven.

Regardless of how much honor and glory I give You, Jesus, I know I can always give more. For that reason I look forward to praising You for all eternity!

The Price of Redemption

*Father, I desire that they also whom You gave Me
may be with Me where I am....*

JOHN 17:24

∾

Lord, I am deeply moved by Your declaration that
You desired for me to live with You in heaven. Even before
I was born You determined to make me Yours, and You
put into action a plan that stopped at nothing to free me
from the clutches of sin.

You knew before You came to earth that You would be
persecuted and reviled. Hated and despised. Condemned
and crucified. You counted the cost...and still You desired
me. You paid much too high a price for me, and You did
it willingly.

Whenever I struggle over the cost of being Your child
in this hostile world, remind me, O Lord, that it is but a
small cost that I should gladly bear.

His Goodness Never Ends

*Blessed be the God and Father of our Lord Jesus
Christ, who according to His abundant mercy has
begotten us again to a living hope…to an inheritance incorruptible….*

1 PETER 1:3-4

∾

I praise You, Father, that because of the cross, the slate
of my life has been wiped clean. No sin—past, present,
or future—can be held against me. You paid the penalty
in full, once and for all.

And Your Son did not stop with salvation. I know "He
always lives to make intercession" for me (Hebrews 7:25).
He watches over and sanctifies and cleanses me so that I
might "be holy and without blemish" (Ephesians 5:27).

And there's still more! I will one day rule with Him in
glory and enjoy "every spiritual blessing in the heavenly
places" (Ephesians 1:3). What a gift You have given me
in Jesus—Your goodness to me never ends!

Fairest Lord Jesus

*Walk in love, as Christ also has loved us
and given Himself for us....*

EPHESIANS 5:2

∽

I praise You, Lord Jesus, for the glorious example You are to me. From You I have learned how to love others with a tender compassion. You were not ashamed to be a friend to sinners or to offer a caring hand to the outcast. You gave comfort to the hurting and hope to the oppressed. With firmness You rebuked Your enemies, yet You did not take vengeance on them.

You came to serve, not to be served. You humbled Yourself to do the Father's will and not Your own. You endured great suffering with patience and fortitude. And You demonstrated that there is no greater love than to lay down one's life for others.

Thank You, dear Lord, for showing me how to live and to serve. May I be a willing follower in Your footsteps.

Responding to His Love

*To Him who loved us and washed us from our
sins in His own blood, and has made us kings and
priests to His God and Father, to Him be glory and
dominion forever and ever. Amen.*

REVELATION 1:5-6

Jesus, as I reflect on the wondrous display of Your love
at the cross, my heart wells up in a gratitude too deep for
words. You endured the worst of mortal suffering so that
I might experience the best of immortal blessing. Because
You submitted to the wrath and fury of Your Father, I am
able to know the blessing and glory of Your Father.

At the outpouring of such love I cannot help but be
moved. Oh, that I would be more devoted to You and
follow You more wholeheartedly! Should temptation
knock at the door of my heart, may I spurn it, for to sin
would be inconsistent with the love I owe to You. Instead,
may everything I say and do be worthy of being lifted up
as an offering of thanksgiving and praise to You.

Love's Redeeming Work Is Done

But God raised Him up again, putting an end to the agony of death, since it was impossible for Him to be held in its power.

Acts 2:24 NASB

∽

Father, how glorious are the words, "He is risen!" I magnify and praise You for Jesus' victory over the grave. With His resurrection, death reigns no more. And because He arose, I too will one day rise. Yes, love's redeeming work is done!

Today Jesus sits at Your right hand, highly exalted "far above all rule and authority, power and dominion" (Ephesians 1:21 NIV). Having died to save me, He now lives to make me holy and to prepare a place for me in heaven. Yes, Christ has opened paradise!

And a day is coming when every knee will bow, and every tongue will confess that Jesus Christ is Lord. He will reign over a new heaven and earth, and I will reign with Him—for all eternity. Yes, I will raise my joys and triumphs high!

The Holy Spirit

Come, holy Comforter,
Thy sacred witness bear
In this glad hour:
Thou who almighty art,
Now rule in every heart,
And ne'er from us depart,
Spirit of power.

ANONYMOUS
"COME, THOU ALMIGHTY KING"

The Ultimate Prayer Partner

*The Spirit also helps in our weaknesses. For we do
not know what we should pray for as we ought, but
the Spirit Himself makes intercession for us with
groanings which cannot be uttered.*

ROMANS 8:26

∽

I exalt You, Lord, for the marvelous work of the
Holy Spirit on my behalf. In my human weaknesses and
limitations, I realize I do not always pray as I should.
Sometimes I don't know Your will for me. Sometimes I am
not aware of my true spiritual need. And sometimes I let
my human desires get in the way of Your divine plan.

Though I may pray with all sincerity, I realize my
requests are flawed at best. And so Your Holy Spirit steps
in and specifies my real needs in accord with His perfect
wisdom and Your perfect will. He says what I am unable
to say. I praise You for giving me such an Advocate—One
who will never cease to sustain and protect me. How
wonderful that You, the Son, and the Spirit are united in
caring for me in more ways than I'll ever know!

Honoring the Guest of Honor

I will pray the Father, and He will give you another
Helper, that He may abide with you forever—the
Spirit of truth....

JOHN 14:16-17

∽

Lord, I find it incredible to know that at the moment of my salvation, Your Holy Spirit came to dwell in me. Your Spirit actually *lives* within me...so that He might enable me to live out my new identity as Your child. Yet at times I forget about His presence, and I grieve or ignore Him. At times He has to nudge my heart repeatedly before I listen to Him.

Dear Holy Spirit, I thank You for Your persistence. Jesus promised You would be my Advocate...and true to His word, You have been my unfailing help. You have guided and sustained me and made Christ real within me. May I always treat You as the Guest of Honor in my life by surrendering my all to receive Your all. Thank You, Holy Spirit, for abiding in me and helping me.

The Spirit's Love for Us

You were sealed with the Holy Spirit of promise,
who is the guarantee of our inheritance....

EPHESIANS 1:13-14

✍

Dear Holy Spirit, You show Your love for me in so many ways! You began by convicting me of my sin and my need for a Savior. At the moment of my salvation You sealed me for eternity, placed me in the body of Christ, and gave me spiritual gifts. You have given me new eyes to reveal the truths of Scripture to me. You dwell in me, pray for me, teach me, bear fruit through me, and are transforming me. And You are preserving me till that glorious day when my mortal body takes on immortality.

Thank You, Holy Spirit, for the many and constant expressions of Your love for me. Thank You for Your unceasing faithfulness.

Our Helper Who Enables Us

When the Helper comes, whom I shall send to you
from the Father...He will testify of Me.

JOHN 15:26

✍

Jesus, what a wonderful Helper the Holy Spirit is! He illumines the Scriptures for me so that I might understand them, and He points my attention to You so that I might learn from and become more like You.

Without the Spirit's light, I would be blind to You and Your truth. And without the Spirit's power, I would be unable to bear His fruit. He enables me to become all that You desire for me to be.

Because of Your Spirit, Lord, I can live victoriously. Thank You for sending Him into my life to dwell within me. May I always walk in Him and yield myself to His filling so that through me, others may see You too.

The Bible

*The Scripture is the standard of truth, the judge of controversies;
it is the pole-star to direct us to heaven....The Scripture is
the compass by which the rudder of our will is to be steered;
it is the field in which Christ, the Pearl of price, is hid;
it is a rock of diamonds; it is a sacred "eye-salve";
it heals their eyes that look upon it; it is a spiritual optic-glass
in which the glory of God is resplendent;
it is the panacea or "universal medicine" for the soul.*[8]

THOMAS WATSON

A Purifying Power

Your word is very pure;
therefore Your servant loves it.

PSALM 119:140

∽

Father, the psalmist tells me Your Word is "*very* pure." It's pure to the point of perfection. That which You have said and written has no fault…no error…no sin. Rather, Your Word is pure in its influence…its wisdom…its counsel. And the more I expose myself to it, the more it washes and cleanses and purges me so that I may become a vessel fit for Your use.

May I delight in, honor, and hunger for Your Word. May I not only know it and cherish it but also practice it. May my obedience to its precepts be so complete that it shapes my every thought, word, and action. May I give myself wholly to Your Word so that it may wholly transform me.

The Perfect Guide

*Your word is a lamp to my feet
and a light to my path.*

PSALM 119:105

∾

Heavenly Father, Your living Word is so very precious to me. All the treasures of the earth cannot purchase for me that which I can receive from Your Word. Only Scripture can convert the soul, make wise the simple, rejoice the heart, enlighten the eyes, warn the heart, and bring eternal reward (Psalm 19:7-8,11). Only Scripture can make me truly complete in the way You intended, giving me instruction and correction that prepares me for every good work (2 Timothy 3:16).

Your Word, Lord, provides counsel for my every need. May I always hunger and thirst for it; may I never tire of mining its riches. What a mighty gift and guide You have given me for all of life!

His Word a Source of Blessing

Your testimonies I have taken as a heritage forever,
for they are the rejoicing of my heart.

PSALM 119:111

❧

I praise You, Lord, that You are a God who desires to communicate with me. Your infinite wisdom and Your perfect will are made available to me at all times in Your beloved Word.

Through the Scriptures I can get to know You intimately…and I can listen as You speak to my heart. I can look back at how You guided and cared for Your children in ages past, knowing that You will provide the same guidance and care for me today. And Your Word is filled to overflowing with truths and promises that, when stored in my heart, are able to encourage and direct me at any moment of the day.

Father, I could never exhaust the treasure You have given me in Your Word. What a source of blessing it is to me!

In Times of Suffering

Fear not, I am with thee; O be not dismayed,
For I am thy God, and will still give thee aid;
I'll strengthen thee, help thee, and cause thee to stand,
Upheld by my righteous omnipotent hand.

ANONYMOUS
"HOW FIRM A FOUNDATION"

His Care Is Constant

…casting all your care upon Him, for He cares for you.

1 PETER 5:7

❦

Dear Father, You lovingly command me to surrender my cares to You. Too often I let the weight of my burdens press me down. Help me to remember that the heaviness on my mind and heart is not heaviness to You at all.

I praise You for Your promise to care for me in every season of life, regardless of how difficult. Though I may not see Your face, I know You are with me even in the darkest of night. Though I may not feel Your presence, I know You are always with me, a very present help in times of trouble.

Too often I see Your loving care only in that which is miraculous or obvious. Help me to see the many quiet and ordinary ways You care for me. Open my eyes to the constant expressions of Your love for me!

Always for Our Best

*Count it all joy when you fall into various trials,
knowing that the testing of your faith produces
patience....that you may be perfect and complete,
lacking nothing.*

JAMES 1:2-4

෴

Heavenly Father, I know You are too wise to ever make a mistake. When something appears to go wrong for me, I know it's not a mere accident.

Regardless of what sufferings I face, I know You have permitted them. Though I may not understand Your plan, help me to rest assured that You know which path I need to walk so I can become everything You desire for me to be. May I not seek to escape Your refining process; rather, may I allow Your purpose in my trial to be accomplished.

I praise You, Lord, that the testing of my faith helps me to grow stronger. Help me to always look ahead to the end result, knowing that even the worst of circumstances can turn out for my best.

The One We Can Count On

...sorrowful, yet always rejoicing....

2 CORINTHIANS 6:10

∽

Dear Lord, thank You for the apostle Paul's loving reminder that even in the midst of sorrow, I can continue to rejoice. Even when life is hard, I can know a deep inner joy...all because of the spiritual blessings You've given to me, which can never be taken away.

Even when life goes wrong, You are a Shepherd who will care for me, a Friend who will stay with me, a Father who will watch over me. You are a Rock who will help me stand firm, a Shield who will protect me from danger, a Counselor who will guide me.

When all else seems lost, I know I can still count on You. Even when I can't think of anything to be thankful for, in reality, I have much to be thankful for. I praise You, Lord, for Your faithfulness to me.

From Despair to Praise

Why are you cast down, O my soul?
And why are you disquieted within me?
Hope in God, for I shall yet praise Him.

PSALM 42:5

✽

Father, too often I come to You grumbling and complaining rather than worshiping and adoring. I can so easily become preoccupied with the ugliness of my circumstances and forget that You have the wisdom and power to create something good and beautiful out of them all.

When my focus is negative, nudge my heart...and remind me to dwell on that which is true, noble, just, pure, lovely, of good report, virtuous, and praiseworthy (Philippians 4:8). Though I may not be able to change that which is around me, I know You can change my heart and my perspective. May I learn the calming hope and peace that comes from praising You even when I don't feel like it.

The Healer of Our Hurts

Out of the depths I have cried to You, O LORD;
Lord, hear my voice!
Let Your ears be attentive
to the voice of my supplications.

PSALM 130:1-2

∽

Lord, You know the hidden sighs of my heart. You know my secret anguish, my silent tears. Your all-seeing eyes perceive the suffering that no one else sees. Though I may hide my grief from those around me, I can hide nothing from You...and for that, I am grateful.

Others may abandon me, but You are always near. Others may misunderstand me, but You don't. Even my own heart deceives me at times, but You will never betray me.

Because You are all-knowing, You alone can comfort and heal me. You alone can guide and restore me. Regardless of the cause of my hurt, You know the way to help me. You are indeed the Great Physician!

Persevering and Praising

Christ also suffered for us, leaving us an example,
that you should follow His steps.

1 PETER 2:21

∽

Dear Lord, You have called me to have a heart filled with rejoicing and praise. Yet in my human frailty, I am all too prone to grumbling and despair.

I thank You that Your Son has already walked the difficult road before me and given me a pattern I can follow. When my heart aches from life's burdens…when I am wounded by those around me…when I am persecuted for righteousness' sake…I need only to remember how Your Son was humiliated, afflicted, rejected, and despised. And through it all, He remained patient, loving, and steadfast—even to the point of death. By comparison, I have suffered little.

May my recollection of Jesus' faithfulness refresh me and give me new strength. Teach me to endure as Jesus did…and to praise You in all things at all times.

The Perspective from Eternity

*For of Him and through Him and to Him are all
things, to whom be glory forever. Amen.*

ROMANS 11:36

❧

Heavenly Father, there is so much of life that I don't understand. You say that all things work together for good to those who love You. Yet at times I feel so overwhelmed by my problems that I can't help but ask…why me? And for what purpose?

I thank You that someday, I will stand with You on the hilltops of glory and look back at the landscape of my life…and I will see more clearly how You used every rough path I walked to polish me and make me more complete. I will see what I didn't see before—that You permitted my trials out of love, You enabled me to endure them, and You used them to bring You honor.

May I not wait until then to praise You for Your perfecting work in me. May I start praising You right now…and trusting all the more Your great faithfulness.

In Times of Worship

O for a thousand tongues to sing
My great Redeemer's praise,
The glories of my God and King,
The triumphs of His grace.

My gracious Master and my God,
Assist me to proclaim,
To spread through all the earth abroad
The honors of Thy name.

CHARLES WESLEY
"O FOR A THOUSAND TONGUES"

The Power of Praise

Praise the LORD!
I will praise the LORD
with my whole heart.

PSALM 111:1

∽

Father, thank You for the gift of praise, which allows me to express my love and adoration to You. Thank You for the special way that praise enriches and elevates the relationship I enjoy with You.

My desire, Lord, is that my praise will always bring joy to You. Even when my heart is downcast…and even when times are hard…may my praise be whole and genuine. Even when I seem to have nothing to be thankful for, remind me that I have much to be grateful for.

Thank You for the way praise can lift my heart and help me view my circumstances in a new light. Thank You for how it can turn a worldly defeat into a spiritual victory!

No Greater Privilege

Serve the LORD with gladness;
come before His presence with singing.

PSALM 100:2

❧

Lord, what is the mood of my heart when I serve You? Am I serving You with gladness or because I have to? Is my service prompted by love or by duty?

Being Your servant is such a privilege! Nothing is ordinary about the work You have called me to. May I always be mindful of whom I serve…and may I find satisfaction in knowing that everything I do for You will bear fruit that lasts for eternity.

My service, O Lord, is but a drop compared to the ocean of blessings You've poured out on me. That is reason enough for me to always serve You with gladness and singing. May my service to You be so attractive that others are able to see more of Your greatness.

He Is Worthy of Praise...Always

I will praise You, O LORD, with my whole heart;
I will tell of all Your marvelous works.
I will be glad and rejoice in You;
I will sing praise to Your name, O Most High.

PSALM 9:1-2

❦

Lord, thank You for the example the psalmist provides in these words. Not once, not twice, but four times he says, "I will." What dedication, to make praise such a high priority!

Help me to praise You not only in the bright days of life but also in the dark nights. And may I give that praise with my whole heart. Though my circumstances may change, I know Your love for me is constant...and therefore my praise ought to be constant too.

From the psalmist I also learn that one way to praise You is to tell of all Your marvelous works. Father, may I always be alert to opportunities to speak of Your care in my life. How will others know of Your greatness unless I proclaim it?

Slow Down and Worship

My voice You shall hear in the morning, O LORD;
in the morning I will direct it to You, and I will look up.

PSALM 5:3

∽

Lord, convict me when I become too busy to praise You when I first wake up. Starting the day with You helps me view everything from Your heavenly perspective rather than my earthly one.

Help me to slow down and marvel over Your great power, which can perform wonders beyond what I can imagine…Your steadfast love, which cares for me regardless of what happens…and Your perfect knowledge, which anticipates my every need from today into eternity.

Remembering how awesome You are makes such a difference! Then I can face the day with boldness rather than fear…peace rather than anxiety…and hope rather than despair.

Glorifying Him Through Our Praise

Whoever offers praise glorifies Me.

PSALM 50:23

∽

Lord, help me to remember at all times that my life is a stage on which other people can see You on display. Each time I share with others how You've blessed me, I am giving them a glimpse of Your greatness. Each time I praise You, I am bringing honor to You.

And Lord, You are so worthy of that honor! You have blessed me far beyond what I deserve. You have raised me up in Christ and given me a spiritual inheritance that will never perish. You have surrounded me with people who care about me. And You have provided for my every need.

As I recount each of Your blessings, Lord, may I declare them to others and bring glory to You.

Celebrating the Gift of Praise

Oh, that men would give thanks to the LORD for His goodness....
For He satisfies the longing soul....

PSALM 107:8-9

∽

Lord, I thank You for gifting me with the ability to know and worship You. I am so blessed to be able to converse with You and exalt You. As I lift up my prayers and gratitude to You, I feel my heart lifted up as well.

When I bow before Your throne in adoration, I sense within me a satisfaction unlike any other. As I magnify Your name, I experience true happiness and contentment.

Thank You for allowing me the privilege of offering up praises to You. May I grow to cherish this privilege and let it permeate every part of my life. I will never have enough days to celebrate Your greatness—not even in eternity!

The Hope of Heaven

When we've been there ten thousand years
Bright shining as the sun,
We've no less days to sing God's praise
Than when we'd first begun.

JOHN NEWTON
"AMAZING GRACE"

Created for Eternity

*God, who is rich in mercy...made us alive together
with Christ...that in the ages to come He might
show the exceeding riches of His grace....*

EPHESIANS 2:4-7

✍

Heavenly Father, as a creature of this earth, I can easily
get caught up in that which is fleeting and temporary.
Remind me that my time here is short and that You have
redeemed me for eternity. May I always be mindful that
this world is not my home and that I am a citizen of a
better world to come.

Help me to not limit my vision and my desires to the
things that will perish. Teach me to set my mind on the
exceeding riches of Your grace—"on things above, not on
things on the earth" (Colossians 3:2). Fortify me to resist
the temptations that will divert me from that which really
counts. May my life *here* always be focused on *eternity!*

The Promise of His Return

When the Son of Man comes in His glory, and all the holy angels with Him, then He will sit on the throne of His glory.

MATTHEW 25:31

℘

Lord, how I love the promise of Your coming! In a world that increasingly rejects You and takes pleasure in wickedness, the assurance of Your return is a blessed hope to which I can hold fast.

In that glorious day, the world that was lost to sin will be won to righteousness. The creation that fell under bondage to corruption will be restored to its full beauty. And Your children will at long last be changed from mortality to immortality.

How I look forward to the time when You will triumph once and for all over sin, pain, hatred, and injustice... and You will rule from Your throne with all glory, power, majesty, and authority!

Living in Anticipation of Heaven

*We, according to His promise, look for new heavens
and a new earth in which righteousness dwells.*

2 PETER 3:13

∽

Father, time and again Your Word reminds me that I am merely a pilgrim here on earth and that my real home is heaven. You urge me to set my affections on the glories above and not the things of earth.

And no wonder! The treasures of earth are but dull trinkets compared to the brilliant jewels of heaven. The happiness and love and contentment I know here are but a faint image of what I will know in my celestial home.

Thank You, Father, for the promise of heaven. In the times when I am weary, may I fix my heart upon the joys that await me in the realms of bliss…knowing that to do so will renew my strength and carry me onward in this journey called life.

The Joy of Heaven

In Your presence is fullness of joy;
at Your right hand are pleasures forevermore.

PSALM 16:11

❧

In Your presence, Lord, is a fullness of joy that will be more satisfying than any I can know here on earth. No more will I endure the wintry storms that cast darkness and hardship upon my path. No more will the havoc wrought by sin rob me of peace and rest.

And this joy will be everlasting—one that will never end. No more will sin ever interrupt my fellowship with You. No more will I ever have to depart from the presence of loved ones and dear saints. No more will I ever live in fear of sorrow, pain, and death.

Lead me through the wilderness, Lord, to the safety of heaven's shores. And along the way, spur me onward with Your promise that "weeping may endure for a night, but joy comes in the morning" (Psalm 30:5).

Destined for Glory

We know that when He is revealed, we shall be like Him, for we shall see Him as He is.

1 JOHN 3:2

෨

Father, on many days I feel like anything but a child of God. I entertain thoughts not pleasing to You, I speak words unbecoming of You, and I carry out actions that bring reproach upon You.

And yet through it all, You still forgive me, keep me, and love me as Your child. With patience and tenderness You continue to refine me more and more into the image of Your Son—till that wonderful day when, at last, I shall be like Him.

I love You, Lord, for Your grace, which has destined me for glory. For Your guidance, which enables my progress. And for Your faithfulness, which will bring me home. You are my hope, my joy, my crown.

*P*raise God from whom all blessings flow,
Praise Him all creatures here below,
Praise Him above, ye heavenly host,
Praise Father, Son, and Holy Ghost.

THOMAS KEN

∽

DOXOLOGY,
FROM "AWAKE MY SOUL, AND WITH THE SUN"

One-Minute
Promises

The Power of God's Promises

There has not failed one word
of all His good promise.

1 Kings 8:56

∽

When God makes a promise, He guarantees it for eternity. Nothing can void or change His Word. Even if the entire universe were wiped out of existence, His Word would still stand, including all the promises within it.

That should give you some idea of the level of confidence you can place in the Lord's promises. They comprise an anchor that is immovable. A foundation that is unshakeable. A mountain that cannot be toppled.

God's promises can stand forever because He Himself will stand forever. The One who made the promises found in the Bible is infinite. Nothing can limit Him. Therefore, nothing can limit His promises. "There has not failed one word of all His good promise" (1 Kings 8:56). Isn't that incredible?

Make use of His promises. When you do, you will see the mightiness of God on display, as will others. And you'll see just how much He loves you.

Love

O love of God, how strong and true!
Eternal and yet ever new;
Uncomprehended and unbought,
Beyond all knowledge and all thought.

HORATIUS BONAR

A Love That Never Diminishes

*God, who is rich in mercy, because of His great love
with which He loved us, even when we were dead
in trespasses, made us alive together with Christ.*

EPHESIANS 2:4-5

∞

Have you ever wondered, *How can God still want me
or love me after the ways I've failed Him?*

Yet God's mercy is so rich and His love is so great
that He loved you even when you were "dead in trespasses." Before you became a Christian, you were lost
in total spiritual darkness—you had nothing redeeming
to offer. Spiritually, you were utterly bankrupt. Even
then, in that depraved state, God reached out to you
in love and called you to Him in salvation so that you
might be made "alive together with Christ."

If He loved you even when you were at your
absolute worst as an unbeliever, then you can do
nothing as a believer that will diminish His love for
you. In fact, His love is not based on your performance.
Yes, you will grieve His heart when you sin. But you
can still count on His love for you, which is constant—
no matter what!

A Tough and Enduring Love

Yes, I have loved you with an everlasting love.

JEREMIAH 31:3

&

Though God gave this promise to ancient Israel, it has very definite significance to us today as well. The story behind this statement reminds us just how much God loves those He calls His own.

This promise came through the prophet Jeremiah, who warned the Israelites of God's anger and imminent punishment in response to their gross idolatry and other wicked practices. Even when God threatened severe judgment, He yearned for His people to repent, and affirmed His love for them.

Just as a parent still loves a rebellious child when punishing him, God loves us even when He must discipline us. We cannot outrun His love, for it is an everlasting love. May we never abuse it or take advantage of it, but rather thank Him for it and show Him our love in return.

A Love You Can Count On

I am persuaded that neither death nor life, nor angels nor principalities nor powers, nor things present nor things to come, nor height nor depth, nor any other created thing, shall be able to separate us from the love of God which is in Jesus Christ our Lord.

ROMANS 8:38-39

❧

God's love for us is so permanent, so indestructible, so everlasting that nothing—absolutely *nothing*—can separate us from it. This promise in Romans 8:38-39 is so all-encompassing that it has no exceptions whatsoever. Nothing can separate you and God.

Note what these verses don't promise. They don't tell us that God will help us to circumvent life's problems. They don't tell us that life is easier for those who are Christians. But God *does* promise He will be our constant companion through the hard times.

That's why, when trouble comes your way, you have nothing to fear. God is always at your side, ready to protect and care for you. Nothing will ever separate you from Him!

A Love That Never Changes

For the mountains shall depart and the hills be removed, but My kindness shall not depart from you, nor shall My covenant of peace be removed.

ISAIAH 54:10

❧

Though the earth may change and mountains disappear, God's love will never depart from His people. Though the forces of change are ever in motion all around us, God's kindness toward us remains constant. As the years pass by and time marches on, His promises to us are steadfast as ever.

God has pledged to love us with an enduring love. Nothing in the past, present, or future can alter that. Nothing will take His love or kindness away from you. What a comforting truth this is...we don't have to live in the fear that we have to earn His love or that we might inadvertently fall out of His favor. Have you expressed your appreciation to Him for this great and everlasting love?

Joy

Why should Christians be such a happy people?
It is good for our God;
it gives Him honor among men when we are glad.
It is good for us; it makes us strong....
It is good for the ungodly; when they see Christians glad,
they long to be believers themselves.
It is good for our fellow Christians;
it comforts them and tends to cheer them.

C.H. SPURGEON

The Source of True Joy

*These things I have spoken to you, that my joy may
remain in you, and that your joy may be full.*

JOHN 15:11

∽

Christ desires that our joy "may be full." Not par-
tial, not fleeting, but full.

The joy Jesus is speaking of is not a jolly cheerful-
ness. Rather, it is an inner happiness and contentment
that doesn't depend on external circumstances. It is the
assurance that God will use all that happens to us for
our ultimate good and for His glory. And because it is
internal, it isn't dependent on other people's actions or
attitudes toward us.

Christ is the giver of joy, and the truths He taught—
especially His promises—were given so that His joy
might remain in us. The joy He gives is a kind that lasts,
a kind that can buoy us upward when crises threaten
to pull us downward.

Joy is not a matter of what's happening *around* you,
but *inside* you. In your heart and mind, are you focused
upon Jesus, His words, His promises? If you are, then
you will know joy.

From Hindrance to Opportunity

Count it all joy when you fall into various trials,
knowing that the testing of your faith produces patience.
But let patience have its perfect work, that you may be
perfect and complete, lacking nothing.

JAMES 1:2-4

∞

If we were to rank the seemingly most irrational statements in the Bible, this one would land near the top of the list. Count it all joy when life seems rotten? How can that possibly make sense?

But James is not talking about artificial smiles and giddy emotions that ignore our difficult circumstances. He's not saying we're to enjoy our trials or that they themselves are joy. Rather, he's saying we can have joy *in the midst* of our troubles. Joy that comes from knowing God is still in control. From knowing that hardships help to purify, strengthen, and mature us. From focusing on things that cannot be taken away from us rather than things that can.

When we view our troubles as opportunities, God can use us more effectively. Is that your heart's desire?

Strength

God is not waiting to show us strong in His behalf,
but Himself strong in our behalf.
That makes a lot of difference.
He is not out to demonstrate
what we can do but what He can do.

VANCE HAVNER

Waiting on the Lord

Wait on the LORD; be of good courage, and He shall strengthen your heart; wait, I say, on the LORD!

PSALM 27:14

❧

Waiting on the Lord is hard to do in our instant age. At the touch of a keyboard, at the push of a button, we can have what we want. But not everything in life works like that. We still have concerns that remain unanswered, worries that have no immediate solutions. These stretch our patience and cause us to become anxious...worried...or even depressed or angry.

The psalmist who wrote, "Wait on the LORD" had faced the challenge of scanning the horizon of life and seeing nothing but dark and threatening storm clouds. His reply? Wait on the Lord. Be patient. After all, He can see into the future, beyond the horizon of our troubles, and we can't. He doesn't expect us to understand, but He invites us to trust Him and wait.

Let us not run ahead of God or act on our own power. Rather, let us wait and stay at His side...and He will strengthen us.

Waiting for the Best Possible Outcome

*Those who wait for the LORD will gain new strength;
they will mount up with wings like eagles, they will run
and not get tired, they will walk and not become weary.*

ISAIAH 40:31 (NASB)

∽

Noah waited 120 years for the flood. Abraham waited decades for his son Isaac. Hannah waited to the point of despair in her want of a son. Nehemiah and his fellow Israelites waited 70 years before their release from Babylon.

In every instance, those who waited on God saw wonderful results. Those who didn't wait made grave mistakes.

At times, waiting may seem the hardest thing in the world to do, but it's actually the easiest. For when we wait, we allow God the freedom to orchestrate our lives and circumstances in ways that bring about the very best possible outcome. Isn't that what we really want?

He Will Lift You Up

Do not fear, for I am with you; do not anxiously look about you, for I am your God. I will strengthen you, surely I will help you. Surely I will uphold you with My righteous right hand.

ISAIAH 41:10 (NASB)

❧

What fears are you struggling with right now? What weighs heavily on your heart? Have you lifted your anxieties up to God and truly let go of them?

We may be weak and frail, but we have a strong and mighty God. He is so great and so powerful that He laid the foundations of the earth and determined the boundaries of the seas (Job 38:4,8), yet He never forgets to feed even the little birds that hunger for food (Matthew 6:26).

And God's promises in Isaiah 41:10 are absolute. They leave no room for exceptions:

I *am* your God.

I *will* strengthen you.

I *will* help you.

I *will* uphold you.

So when you find yourself being pulled down, look to God...and He will lift you up.

Nothing Is Too Hard

Is anything too hard for the LORD?

GENESIS 18:14

❧

How powerful is God?

Powerful enough to create the entire universe merely by speaking. To cover the entire globe in a flood. To part the Red Sea and close it up again. To feed and water two million Israelites every single day as they wandered through the wilderness for 40 years. To crumble the seemingly indomitable walls of Jericho with the sound of trumpets. To bring the Babylonian captivity to an end after 70 years, exactly as promised. To cause a virgin to give birth. To walk on water. To calm the violent winds and waves on the Sea of Galilee. To heal the blind, the deaf, the lame. To feed thousands from a few loaves of bread. To go to the cross with joy. And the crowning achievement on our behalf, to conquer the previously unconquerable grip of death.

Are you facing a situation too hard for you to handle? Give it to the Lord. Let Him take care of it. As we've just seen, nothing is too hard for Him.

Help in the Midst of Hardship

We are hard-pressed on every side, yet not crushed;
we are perplexed, but not in despair; persecuted,
but not forsaken; struck down, but not destroyed.

2 CORINTHIANS 4:8-9

∽

In every hardship we face, we can be absolutely certain God will preserve us. We may wonder about the limits of our endurance, but God promises never to let us reach the breaking point.

But why does God even allow us to face trials? Wouldn't we achieve more if we didn't have to struggle so much?

When all is well, we are much more likely to forget God. We have little or no reason to seek His help. But when the storms strike, we are compelled to draw closer to Him—which is where He wants us.

Someone once said, "Trials are not intended to break us but to make us." Difficulties *are* beneficial—they help us to grow stronger and wiser, and to plant our roots more deeply in the bedrock of God Himself.

Eternal Life

*One thought of eternity makes
all earthly sorrows fade away.*

BASILIA SCHLINK

The Best Guarantee Ever

*Most assuredly, I say to you, he who believes in Me
has everlasting life.*

JOHN 6:47

❧

Almost nothing is 100 percent sure in life. Things
break. Time runs out. Investments go sour. Plans go
awry. People break promises. Weather changes. Friends
betray us. Loved ones hurt us. Coworkers don't follow
through. Our health deteriorates. Modern technology
doesn't stay modern. Tornadoes, hurricanes, floods,
and earthquakes destroy in an instant that which has
taken a lifetime to build.

But we Christians have one guarantee we can
always count on. It will never change. No one can ever
take it away from us. Nothing can ever happen to it.

That's the gift of eternal life. Eternal, as in forever
and ever. A perfect life, in the presence of a perfect
God, in the midst of perfect peace, perfect love, and
perfect joy.

Life's problems *will* come to an end. And someday,
we *will* enjoy eternal life.

It's guaranteed!

The Ultimate Makeover

If anyone is in Christ, he is a new creation; old things have passed away; behold, all things have become new.

2 CORINTHIANS 5:17

∞

Nothing is more radical than becoming a Christian. Believers have moved from death to life. From darkness to light. From rebellion to obedience. From despair to hope. From hatred to love. From turmoil to peace. From condemnation to acceptance. From hell to heaven.

Yes, the old things have passed away, and all things have become new. *All* things! You now have Christ, who promises to be with you always. You now have the Holy Spirit, who is your Counselor and Comforter. You have every single promise offered in God's Word—promises of protection, strength, wisdom, peace, deliverance, and victory. And you have everything that heaven has to offer—an eternal inheritance waiting for you. It's the ultimate makeover, the best package deal ever. And it's *all* given to *every* single Christian... including you!

An Accomplished Fact

*Most assuredly, I say to you, he who hears My word
and believes in Him who sent Me has everlasting
life, and shall not come into judgment, but has passed
from death into life.*

JOHN 5:24

In the song "It Is Well with My Soul," Horatio Gates
Spafford wrote,

My sin—O, the bliss of this glorious thought—
My sin, not in part but the whole,
Is nailed to the cross and I bear it no more.
Praise the Lord, praise the Lord, O my soul!

Yes, *all* our sin was nailed to the cross. *None* of it
condemns us anymore. We who are Christians *have*
passed from death to life. Nothing can change the ver-
dict. The phrase "has passed" is in the perfect tense,
indicating an accomplished fact. We won't have any
unexpected surprises regarding our destiny. After all,
eternal life wouldn't be eternal if we could lose it.

How can we possibly thank God enough? As the
song exclaims, "Praise the Lord, praise the Lord, O my
soul!"

Forgiveness

Release! Signed in tears, sealed in blood,
written on heavy parchment,
recorded in eternal archives. The black ink
of the indictment is written all over
with the red ink of the cross:
"The blood of Jesus Christ cleanseth us from all sin."

T. DE WITT TALMAGE

Ready to Forgive

For you, Lord, are good, and ready to forgive, and
abundant in mercy to all those who call upon You.

PSALM 86:5

⤞

Are you doubting whether God will really forgive
you this time? After making yet the same mistake again?
Perhaps you feel as if His patience with you has surely
worn out by now.

But God is not like us human beings, who sometimes take sinister delight in withholding forgiveness
from others. No, God is always "ready to forgive, and
abundant in mercy." When we've wronged Him, He is
eager for us to seek reconciliation with Him. He takes
pleasure in our companionship and our dependence on
Him. And it all starts by calling on Him—that is,
turning away from that which offends Him.

Are you truly sorry? Do you desire for all to be
right between you and Him? If your answer is yes, He
will forgive you!

The Great Escape

In Him we have redemption through His blood, the
forgiveness of sins, according to the riches of His grace.

EPHESIANS 1:7

✍

Imagine, for a moment, what life would be like if you had absolutely no choice but to spend eternity in hell. That would make life pretty bleak, wouldn't it? An utterly total absence of hope and joy. And an overwhelming sense of despair at being unable to reverse your downward descent toward an inescapable and horrible destiny.

Praise God—that's not the case! While we were totally helpless to escape the shackles of sin, Christ paid the required ransom for our release from bondage. He died so that we might live, and He became sin for us that we might become the righteousness of God in Him (2 Corinthians 5:21).

We have been redeemed and forgiven, and we have an incredible future to look forward to—thanks to His wonderful grace!

Gone!

*As far as the east is from the west, so far has He
removed our transgressions from us.*

PSALM 103:12

∽

When God forgives, He forgives so completely and
so totally that we have no reason to ever return to the
past and punish ourselves through feelings of guilt and
regret. He has removed our transgressions "as far as
the east is from the west." What does that mean?

Consider this: If you travel north, eventually you
will reach the top of the globe, where you cannot help
but start traveling south again. You can't travel north
forever. Or south. But you *can* travel to the east or the
west forever—and that's how far God has removed your
sins from you.

Have you made a terrible mistake you just can't get
over? If you've approached God with a sincerely repentant heart and asked Him for forgiveness, you have it
already. The slate is wiped clean, the offense is gone...
forever.

Faithful to Forgive

If we confess our sins, He is faithful and just to forgive us our sins and to cleanse us from all unrighteousness.

1 JOHN 1:9

∞

We have a God who doesn't hold grudges. When we come to Him with a genuinely repentant heart asking for forgiveness, He doesn't say, "I need some time to think about it." No—His forgiveness is immediate, and His cleansing is whole.

And regardless of how great your sin is, God's forgiveness is greater. Don't make the mistake of thinking you've gone beyond the point of being forgivable. Don't accept Satan's invitation to throw a pity party for yourself or listen to his accusations that you have no hope and that you're unworthy of God's love.

As C.H. Spurgeon said, "You sin as a finite creature, but the Lord forgives as the infinite Creator." So don't let the past haunt you. Instead, live thankfully in God's forgiveness.

Amazing Grace

I, even I, am He who blots out your transgressions
for My own sake; and I will not remember your sins.

ISAIAH 43:25

∽

God knows our hearts far better than we do. He knows our every fault, our every weakness. He knows the sins that have taken place in the deepest and most secret recesses of our minds and hearts. He knows every sin we have yet to commit in the future. He knows our entire rap sheet, from birth to death. We can hide nothing from Him.

And yet He still chose to extend the gift of salvation to us. He still chose to make forgiveness available through the Savior, Jesus Christ. In spite of our failures, He stands ready to blot them out and not remember them. No wonder we call this amazing grace!

As a Christian, be sure to never forget where you came from and how God has changed you. Won't you take a moment to thank Him now?

No Condemnation

There is therefore now no condemnation to those who are in Christ Jesus.

ROMANS 8:1

✑

The Bible calls Satan "the accuser" (Revelation 12:10). And no wonder—he works overtime to make us feel guilty about our past. "You're no good," he whispers. "You call yourself a Christian? What about those lustful thoughts in your mind? That gossip you helped to spread? The lie you told at work?" And when you do something *really* stupid, Satan gleefully chuckles, "No way is God gonna forgive you for *that!*"

But your salvation was a gift given on the basis of God's grace. You did nothing to obtain it, and you cannot do anything to lose it. Once you're in Christ Jesus, nothing can condemn you. He has paid for every sin in your life—past, present, and future. So no one can hold any sin against you—ever. Christ's sacrifice covers it all.

So when you've already confessed a specific sin to God and you're still haunted by it, don't pay attention to Satan's accusations. God has forgiven you...so don't withhold forgiveness from yourself!

Wisdom

*Wisdom opens the eyes
both to the glories of heaven
and to the hollowness of earth.*

J.A. MOTYER

The Great Counselor

I, wisdom....love those who love me, and those who seek me diligently will find me.

PROVERBS 8:12,17

❦

Some decisions are simple and don't require much thought. And when we just can't make up our minds, we'll flip a coin or let a friend make the choice for us.

But occasionally we face decisions of greater significance—those that require a lot of us or have a long-term consequence. Should we, or shouldn't we? Which is the better of two options? Sometimes we'll vacillate to the point of agony, unsure of what to do.

When we can't make up our minds, or we're just not sure, we have no better Counselor to go to than God Himself. Proverbs 2:6 says, "The LORD gives wisdom; from His mouth come knowledge and understanding." When you have a decision to make, bring it to Him and leave it at His feet. Keep it before Him in prayer and ask Him to lead you. His perfect and infinite wisdom is more than adequate for even the biggest decisions we face.

Unlimited Wisdom

*If any of you lacks wisdom, let him ask of God,
who gives to all liberally and without reproach,
and it will be given to him.*

JAMES 1:5

∽

If we lack wisdom? Given a choice between human wisdom and divine, we should rush to our knees in perpetual prayer for the latter!

God puts no limit to the wisdom we can ask for. Rather, He "gives to all liberally." We can never cry out to Him too many times. God is not the stern schoolmaster who barks, "When will you ever learn?" Rather, He is the patient Father who says, "I'm glad you asked!"

James 1:5 refers to wisdom in the context of life's trials. Too often we see our problems as hindrances. But they're actually opportunities to seek wisdom. And in the very act of asking, we draw ourselves closer to God—yet another benefit of experiencing troubles.

God asks no price for His priceless wisdom. It's free. Simply ask...and He will give.

Peace

Peace comes not from the absence of troubles,
but from the presence of God.

ALEXANDER MACLAREN

Our Source of Peace

*You will keep him in perfect peace, whose mind is
stayed on You, because he trusts in You.*

ISAIAH 26:3

∼

The opposite of peace is anxiety. We usually experience anxiety when we're uncertain about the future, concerned about meeting our needs, or faced with danger. And when we allow worries to eat away at us, we are failing to trust God to carry us through.

To really trust God means to believe that He can see into the future and that nothing will take Him by surprise. To believe that He knows our every need and will provide. To believe that His power is greater than any danger that might threaten us.

Do you believe? Is your mind "stayed" on God—in other words, is your trust fixed on Him constantly? If so, then you will know "perfect peace." You will know the freedom that comes from totally resting in God and trusting Him to care for you.

Which Will You Choose?

The LORD will give strength to His people; the LORD will bless His people with peace.

PSALM 29:11

∽

When troubles first come along, our inclination is to tackle them head-on without giving much thought to asking God for help. Not until they get worse and overwhelm us do we cry out to our heavenly Father in despair. Instead of looking to Him at the first instant, we turn to Him only as a last resort.

Why do we attempt to rely on human weakness when we can call on divine strength? Why do we exhaust ourselves through worry when we can have peace? We can choose between fighting the stormy seas on our own or resting in the harbor of His strength and peace.

At the first hint of trouble, flee to God. Psalm 29:11 promises that He *will* give you strength and He *will* bless you with peace.

Peace Even in the Midst of Chaos

*Peace I leave with you, My peace I give to you....
Let not your heart be troubled, neither let it be
afraid.*

JOHN 14:27

⌒

Jesus spoke these words to the disciples shortly
before leaving them. He knew that their world would
soon turn upside down and that they would be filled
with fear in response to His crucifixion and His depar-
ture to return to the Father. He encouraged them, in
advance of this tumultuous upheaval, not to be afraid
but to rest in His peace.

One of the many names for Jesus in the Bible is
"Prince of Peace" (Isaiah 9:6). Someday, He will return
to earth and establish His kingdom of peace. Yet we
don't need to wait until then to know His peace. He
offers it to us right now in the midst of life's chaos and
crises. He promised, "I am with you always, even to the
end of the age" (Matthew 28:20). Because He is present
within us, His peace is constantly available to us...and
we need only to ask Him for it.

Exchanging Worry for Peace

*Be anxious for nothing, but in everything by prayer
and supplication, with thanksgiving, let your requests
be made known to God; and the peace of God, which
surpasses all understanding, will guard your hearts
and minds through Christ Jesus.*

PHILIPPIANS 4:6-7

∽

What an incredible offer—our worries in exchange
for God's peace! It's actually more than an offer; it's a
command. When we worry, we are doubting God—we
are questioning His ability to control the outcome of
our circumstances, His timing, His ability to care for us
and intervene on our behalf.

Worry cannot change a thing. But God can. That's
why our heavenly Father lovingly encourages us to
yield all our cares to Him. He doesn't call us to understand, but rather to trust. And when we surrender our
concerns to Him, He will fill us with a peace that calms
us, lifts us above the turmoils of life, and tells a
watching world, "My God is a mighty God, and He will
carry me through this."

A Trust That Leads to Peace

*Great peace have those who love Your law, and
nothing causes them to stumble.*

PSALM 119:165

∽

When we have a true love for God's Word, we will
know true peace. When we rest in the commands and
assurances of Scripture, we will experience rest in our
hearts.

On a human level, when we love someone, we
believe what they say and we *trust* what they do. We
have *confidence* that person has our best interests at
heart.

Do you believe what God says about the afflictions
of life and how they can strengthen us? Do you trust
Him in both good times and bad? Do you have confidence that *all* things work together for good, and not
just some? Can you accept the hard sayings of Scripture without question?

If you can answer yes, you will have peace and not
stumble. May we seek to not only read and understand
God's Word but also love and believe it!

Peace in the Storm

He who dwells in the shelter of the Most High will rest in the shadow of the Almighty. I will say of the LORD, "He is my refuge and my fortress, my God, in whom I trust."

PSALM 91:1-2 (NIV)

∽

We live in a stormy world. We're surrounded by the raging seas and violent winds of broken relationships, workplace pressures, and difficult circumstances. We grow weary as we struggle to endure in the midst of anxiety, discouragement, and hurt. At times we may feel as if the storm has become a hurricane, and nothing is going right. We want to escape it all, but so incessant are the rains and squalls that we lose hope.

At times like these, we can look to the promise that when we seek shelter in God, we can rest in His shadow. He is our refuge, our hiding place. He is our fortress, our shield of protection. He is the quiet harbor in which we can find true peace. When life seems to spin out of control, we can find security in knowing He has complete control over life itself. He doesn't ask us to understand our circumstances; He asks only that we trust Him.

Security

*Security is not the absence of danger
but the presence of God,
no matter what the danger.*

ANONYMOUS

The Certainty of Future Glory

For whom He foreknew, He also predestined to be conformed to the image of His Son....Moreover whom He predestined, these He also called; whom He called, these He also justified; and whom He justified, these he also glorified.

ROMANS 8:29-30

❧

Did you notice that the very last word in Romans 8:30—the word *glorified*—is in the past tense?

If you're a Christian, these verses describe you. You have been predestined, called, and justified, and you *will* be glorified. So definite is this last fact that the apostle Paul wrote it in the past tense even though it hasn't happened yet.

These words are a wonderful testimony of how secure we are in Christ. From the time we were predestined—before the foundation of the world, according to Ephesians 1:4-5—to the time we are glorified in heaven, we are firmly in God's grasp. Not a single one of us will be lost somewhere along the way. As Jesus said in John 10:29, no one is able to snatch us out of the Father's hand. We have nothing to fear; our place in heaven is secure.

A Strong Tower

You have been a shelter for me, a strong tower from the enemy.

PSALM 61:3

⁓

In Bible times, people built towers along city walls to help stabilize them and to provide a city's residents with places of defense and refuge. Towers, then, had a key role in protecting cities and their inhabitants from marauding enemies.

But a tower was effective only as long as people stayed within its strong walls. Those who wandered away did so at their own risk and became extremely vulnerable targets.

God is our tower, and as long as we remain in His shelter—by staying near to Him, living in obedience to Him, fleeing to Him instead of away from Him when we are tempted—we will have His protection.

The enemy can't defeat us unless we make ourselves vulnerable. God has promised you protection, and *nothing* has the power to thwart His care for you.

An Ever-Attentive Father

*The eyes of the LORD are on the righteous, and His
ears are open to their prayers.*

1 PETER 3:12

✐

It happens more often than you like to recount. As
you first wake up, you're already overwhelmed by the
burden of the many responsibilities demanding your
attention. You have more than enough troubles and
not enough time. You wonder how you're going to
make it through the day.

When we're at our busiest, we are most in need of
a few quiet moments to give the day to God. We need
to set aside our self-sufficiency and ask for His super-
natural strength. To yield our anxiety and ask for His
peace. And to lift our concerns to Him rather than sup-
press them within.

God is watching over you, and He's ready to hear
you. With His help, you can make it through the day.
He will enable you to accomplish what you need to get
done. Rest in Him...and your day will go much better.

Treasures Waiting in Heaven for You

*[You have] an inheritance incorruptible and unde-
filed and that does not fade away, reserved in heaven
for you.*

1 PETER 1:4

∽

Chances are, you've lived long enough to know the
pain that comes from the loss of a possession you dearly
treasured. And you've seen that the things of earth do
not last forever. They wear out, break down, or get lost
or stolen. And someday, when you die, the riches you
worked so hard to acquire will end up in the hands of
others. You can't take anything with you to heaven.

Yet you are rich with spiritual possessions that are
waiting for you in heaven at this very moment. Among
them are God Himself, the Lord Jesus Christ, eternal
life, and perfect and everlasting rest, joy, and peace.
These "possessions" will never rust or be destroyed.
They can never be stolen, nor will they fade away with
the passage of time.

Earthly riches don't last; heavenly riches do. To
which are you devoting your attention?

Forever Secure

I give [my sheep] eternal life, and they shall never perish; no one can snatch them out of my hand. My Father, who has given them to me, is greater than all; no one can snatch them out of my Father's hand.

JOHN 10:28-29 (NIV)

○○○

Here we find four great promises for believers: 1) We possess eternal life, 2) we will never perish, 3) no one can snatch us out of God's hand, and 4) God is greater than all. Note that Jesus repeats the promise that no one can take us away. We are forever secure in the hands of both Jesus and the Father.

If you've ever been anxious that somehow you might lose your salvation, worry no more. Because God is "greater than all," nothing is powerful enough to loosen us from His grip. Because we "shall never perish," nothing can steal our assurance that we will one day live in God's presence forever.

Satan wants us to doubt our eternal security so that we live in fear and trepidation. But God has proclaimed His promises to us so we can live in confidence and joy.

Becoming a Finished Masterpiece

*I thank my God...being confident of this very thing,
that He who has begun a good work in you will complete it until the day of Jesus Christ.*

PHILIPPIANS 1:3,6

∽

How many projects have you started but never
gotten around to finishing? In every case, you undoubt-
edly started out with the best of intentions. But eventually, for one reason or another, the projects went to
the wayside.

At the moment of your salvation, God began a
project in you. He desires for you to grow spiritually
mature and become more like Christ. This transfor-
mation is ongoing for the rest of your life. At no step
along the way will God set you aside or give up on
you. His work in you will continue every moment of
every day. You might not notice the growth, but He
promises that He *will* nurture you and that He *will* carry
that work to completion. And by the time you enter
eternity, you will be a finished masterpiece.

He Enables, We Enjoy

Now to Him who is able to keep you from stumbling,
and to present you faultless before the presence of His
glory with exceeding joy...be glory and majesty, do-
minion and power.

JUDE 24-25

∽

Are you giving all the credit where it's due?

Whatever you are able to do in the Christian life, you can do because of God—because of His empowerment, His wisdom, His strength, His everything. He is the One who keeps us from falling, and He enables us to stand in righteousness. Because of what He did through Jesus Christ, we will live in His presence someday and experience eternal bliss.

When you find yourself taking credit for an accomplishment, don't forget who really made it possible. And when others praise you for a job well done, pass that same praise along to God. *He* is the One who enables you. And yet He graciously allows you to fully enjoy the benefits that result from His work in you!

Deliverance

Fear not, I am with thee; O be not dismayed,
For I am thy God and will still give thee aid;
I'll strengthen thee, help thee, and cause thee to stand,
Upheld by my righteous omnipotent hand.

FROM THE HYMN "HOW FIRM A FOUNDATION"

Victory Is Always Possible

He who is in you is greater than he who is in the world.

1 JOHN 4:4

❧

Satan is a tireless foe. He is thoroughly committed to making life as difficult as possible for God's children, throwing every weapon he has in our path in the hopes of hindering us or causing us to stumble. Though he knows he can never have us back, he figures he may as well render us as ineffective as possible.

But we have no reason to be afraid, for Satan is a finite, created being, and we belong to the infinite, almighty Creator-God who is all-powerful, all-knowing, and all present. By contrast, Satan has none of those attributes. He's no match against God.

Yes, the battles we face may become fierce at times. But the Lord who won a decisive and permanent victory at the cross is the same Lord who lives in our hearts. And because He dwells in us, He can help us prevail against the one who is in the world.

A Loyal Protection

The eyes of the LORD run to and fro throughout the whole earth, to show Himself strong on behalf of those whose heart is loyal to Him.

2 CHRONICLES 16:9

∽

In ages past, the role of a king was to protect his loyal subjects. However, if a citizen chose to rebel against the king or journey outside the boundaries of the kingdom, the king's promise of protection no longer applied.

We find a similar promise in the Bible: Those who are loyal to God can count on His protective care. If a problem arises in your life, God is aware of it. No crisis, no tragedy in your life will ever catch God off guard. He sees all and knows all. And regardless of how overwhelming your problem is, it cannot overwhelm God.

For the moment, you may find yourself forced to your knees in dependence on the Lord and crying out in prayer, but ultimately, God will bring deliverance. When we remain loyal to God, He will remain loyal to us—with a fierce tenacity that will carry us to victory.

More than Conquerors

In all these things we are more than conquerors through Him who loved us.

ROMANS 8:37

❧

The Bible says that we who are Christians are more than conquerors...*through Him*.

Perhaps the most significant sense in which we are conquerors is that we can resist temptation and sin. Before salvation, we had no choice. But in Christ, we can refuse to yield the parts of our bodies as "instruments of unrighteousness" and instead present them as "instruments of righteousness" (Romans 6:13).

You can overcome your anger...through Him. Your lust...through Him. Your covetousness...through Him. Your bitterness...through Him. Your victory over any kind of sin is possible only because of Christ's victory on the cross. To mortify your sin, you must go to Him who mortified sin at Calvary.

Do you want to be more than a conqueror? Go to Him. He has already secured the victory for you.

Making the Impossible Possible

Be strong and of good courage, do not fear nor be afraid of them; for the LORD your God, He is the One who goes with you. He will not leave you nor forsake you.

DEUTERONOMY 31:6

∽

This was God's command to the nation of Israel before they crossed the Jordan into the Promised Land. The Israelites were about to face huge armies that had powerful weapons, and God wanted the people of Israel to place their confidence in Him—not in themselves or their woefully inadequate fighting gear.

When we face an overwhelming challenge, our initial response is often discouragement or fear. But even if defeat seems certain, remember this: That which seems impossible to us is always possible with God.

He stands before us in the battle, taking the enemy's blows and clearing a safe path on which we can follow. He will never withdraw His help, and though the heat of the fighting may cause us to momentarily waver or stumble, ultimately, victory belongs to the Lord—and to us.

Deliverance from Temptation

No temptation has overtaken you except such as is common to man; but God is faithful, who will not allow you to be tempted beyond what you are able, but with the temptation will also make the way of escape, that you may be able to bear it.

1 CORINTHIANS 10:13

&

One key reason we look forward to living in heaven is that we won't have to struggle against temptation anymore.

But while we're still on this earth, we can take great comfort in the two guarantees found in 1 Corinthians 10:13: We will *never* experience a temptation greater than we can resist, and God will *always* provide a way of escape.

The spiritual power you have within you is greater than any temptation that might attempt to seduce you. "The Lord is faithful, and He will strengthen and protect you from the evil one" (2 Thessalonians 3:3 NASB).

When you are tempted, do you succumb to the temporary satisfaction sin offers? Or do you run to the Lord for strength to resist? The power is available...you must choose whether you use it.

Waiting with Open Arms

Let us therefore come boldly to the throne of grace,
that we may obtain mercy and find grace to help in
time of need.

HEBREWS 4:16

∽

At the time these words were written, the concept of approaching a king's throne boldly was radical. People just didn't do that. People approached kings with trepidation and fear because displeasing them, even slightly, could mean death.

Yet God, who sits on the highest and most powerful throne of all, is the humblest and most approachable King of all. Earthly rulers might hold their subjects at a distance with disdain, but the heavenly Ruler welcomes His children affectionately with love.

Hebrews 4:16 was written in the context of temptation. Are you struggling? Are you embarrassed or reluctant to call to the Lord for help? Rest assured, no grace can exceed His; no mercy can surpass His. You have no better place to go for help than to Him. So when temptation strikes, *run* to Him. He's waiting with open arms.

Nothing to Fear

"Oh Death, where is your sting? O Hades, where is your victory?" The sting of death is sin, and the strength of sin is the law. But thanks be to God, who gives us the victory through our Lord Jesus Christ.

1 CORINTHIANS 15:55-57

∽

Because of Jesus Christ's work on the cross and in the resurrection, death no longer has the power to end your life. Death is no longer the permanent silencer; rather, God has permanently silenced it.

What's more, for the Christian, death is not the end but the beginning. It's the start of life without affliction, without pain, without temptation, without sin. Death removes us from the land of the dying and takes us to the land of the living.

While the apostle Paul was in prison facing possible death, he proclaimed that "to die is gain" (Philippians 1:21). He then said he had "a desire to depart and be with Christ, which is far better" (verse 23).

Truly, the believer has no reason to fear death. Thanks to Christ, tragedy has turned to triumph, and mortality has turned to immortality. What a victory indeed!

Help in Every Affliction

Many are the afflictions of the righteous, but the
Lord delivers him out of them all.

PSALM 34:19

∽

The word "many" in that verse isn't very comforting, is it? We can expect *numerous* afflictions. Persecution, trials, and troubles are guaranteed in this world. Knowing that, we cannot help but wonder: If God promises to deliver us, then why do we experience affliction in the first place?

Our Father's promise of deliverance does not mean He will remove us from life's problems altogether. Rather, He will *preserve* us through them. Though we may suffer scratches and bruises, we will not be destroyed. Though we may endure loneliness and misunderstandings, we will not be forsaken. Though we can be certain of difficulties, we can be equally certain God will help us in *every* affliction, for He promises to deliver us "out of them *all*." And the ultimate deliverance is still ahead of us—our journey home to heaven, where we will never experience affliction again.

Power

*Surely our greatest trouble in the Christian life is our failure
to realize that God is not as man. The greatest sin of every
Christian, and the Christian Church in general, is to limit the
eternal, absolute power of God to the measure of our own
minds and concepts and understandings.*

MARTYN LLOYD-JONES

The Source for a Productive Life

I am the vine, you are the branches. He who abides in Me, and I in him, bears much fruit; for without Me you can do nothing.

JOHN 15:5

∽

Deep within our nature is a desire to have a real and significant purpose in life. And when we become Christians, that desire becomes more refined—we want to live productively for God and bear fruit for His kingdom.

The secret to such fruitfulness is remarkably simple, yet it requires discipline. Jesus promised that when we abide in Him, we will bear "much fruit." To abide implies intimacy, closeness, a constant pursuing after. Do you draw near to Him daily? Do you spend time in His Word? Do you yield yourself completely to Him? This is all that He asks—He doesn't require us to have a theology degree or years of training. He doesn't expect us to bear fruit in our own power. He produces all the results. We need only to remain close to Him so He can work through us.

Freedom from Fear

*God has not given us a spirit of fear, but of power
and of love and of a sound mind.*

2 TIMOTHY 1:7

✑

If you are facing a trial or threat that has instilled
fear in your heart, that fear didn't come from God. He
has given you everything you need to respond effectively to whatever comes your way in life.

You have power: Ephesians 3:20 says He "is able to
do exceedingly abundantly above all that we ask or
think, according to the power that works in us."

You have love: the kind of love that does not lash out
in anger or vengeance toward the people or circumstances who have caused your fear. "Love your enemies, bless those who curse you, do good to those who
hate you, and pray for those who spitefully use you and
persecute you" (Matthew 5:44).

You have a sound mind: with the help of the Spirit
and the Word, you can respond in a clearheaded
manner rather than with confusion. "If any of you lacks
wisdom, let him ask of God" (James 1:5).

Companionship

The soul that on Jesus hath leaned for repose,
I will not, I will not desert to his foes,
That soul, though all hell should endeavor to shake,
I'll never, no never, no never forsake.

FROM THE HYMN "HOW FIRM A FOUNDATION"

Always Near

He Himself has said, "I will never leave you nor forsake you."

HEBREWS 13:5

∽

Have you felt distant from the Lord lately? Or wondered if He's even listening to your prayers? If so, you don't need to worry that God has moved away or abandoned you. Your emotions or thoughts may betray you and tell you He's far away, but the Bible assures us He's as near as He's ever been.

So emphatic is this promise that the original Greek text contains multiple negatives. Together, they drive home the point that for God to ever leave us is absolutely impossible.

When life doesn't go our way, we may find ourselves wanting to give up on God, to shut Him out of our lives. Fortunately, God will never return the favor. He will remain faithful to us. May we never for a moment want to stray away from Him!

His Devotion to You

Draw near to God and He will draw near to you.

JAMES 4:8

∽

How easily we are distracted from God! When we pray, our minds wander far from spiritual matters. When we attempt to read His Word regularly, we allow ourselves to be pulled away by "urgent" tasks that "must" get done. Though we know our true treasures are in heaven, we oftentimes become more preoccupied with the riches of earth. And when temptation beckons us, instead of fleeing toward God, we linger, not really wanting to say no to the bait dangling before us.

The verses preceding James 4:8 mention those who seek friendship with the world and the fulfillment of their own pleasures. But God jealously yearns for the devotion of those who are His own...and James 4:8 stands as a promise that when we come back to Him with a genuine desire to seek and submit to Him alone, He will welcome us with open arms.

Have you been a wandering sheep lately? Do you need to come back to a closer walk with the Good Shepherd? Draw near to Him, and He will draw near to you.

At Your Side

When you pass through the waters, I will be with you; and through the rivers, they shall not overflow you. When you walk through the fire, you shall not be burned, nor shall the flame scorch you.

ISAIAH 43:2

∽

One of the unfortunate myths that has persisted among believers is that life as a Christian is supposed to be free of problems and pain. But the Bible never says that. Here, we read that we will pass through the waters and rivers, through the fire and flames.

But as we do, God promises to be with us and that nothing will completely overtake us. We may struggle against the swift current of life or even stumble into the water, but we'll never drown. We may feel the intense heat of life's trials, but they will never destroy us. God will enable us to survive through every peril till that day of final redemption. That is why the psalmist could say with confidence, "The LORD is on my side; I will not fear" (Psalm 118:6).

Feeling Special

I am with you always, even to the end of the age.

MATTHEW 28:20

❧

We often envy those who have the rare fortune to know a famous person. And yet as a Christian, you have a personal relationship with the King of kings and Lord of lords Himself. Talk about connections!

And each word of His promise to you in Matthew 28:20 is packed with incredible truth:

I—Jesus Himself, not a stand-in or substitute

am—as in *really* and *right now* with you—not maybe or possibly

with—He's closer than a friend or brother and will never desert you.

you—You're the one! He cares about *you*.

always—every single moment, every single day... from now till eternity

Indeed, His name is Immanuel, which means "God with us." Not symbolically, but literally. *He* made that choice. Doesn't that make you feel pretty special?

Goodness

*It is not enough that we acknowledge
God's infinite resources; we must believe also
that He is infinitely generous to bestow them.*

A.W. TOZER

A Perfect Father

*To all who received him, to those who believed in his
name, he gave the right to become children of God.*

JOHN 1:12 (NIV)

❧

Human parents who love their children do everything they can to meet their needs and oftentimes make personal sacrifices for them. And the same is true about God, to an even greater extent: He promises to meet our every true need, and He made an enormous personal sacrifice on our behalf—one that no one could ever match.

Maybe at times you've doubted God's goodness. But consider the contrast the Bible makes between human parents and our heavenly Parent: "If you then, being evil [that is, imperfect and fallen], know how to give good gifts to your children, how much more will your Father who is in heaven give good things to those who ask Him!" (Matthew 7:11).

God is a perfect Father who cares for His children with a perfect love. And we are His beloved. Have you noticed the fatherly care He has shown to you today?

Two Constant Companions

Surely goodness and mercy shall follow me all the days of my life; and I will dwell in the house of the LORD forever.

PSALM 23:6

∽

On every single day of our journey toward heaven, we have two constant companions: God's goodness and His mercy. Because of His goodness the apostle Paul could say, "My God shall supply *all* your need according to His riches" (Philippians 4:19). And because of His mercy we can say, "There is therefore now no condemnation to those who are in Christ Jesus" (Romans 8:1).

God gives all that we need (that's His goodness), and He takes away all our sins (that's His mercy). He is our abundant Provider and our able Protector. He sustains us and sanctifies us. And because He is forever faithful, His goodness and mercy will continue without fail...forever.

The Proof of His Love

The LORD is good, a stronghold in the day of trouble.

NAHUM 1:7

❧

Many of the troubles we face in life are beyond our comprehension. "Why did God allow that?" we ask. "What good can possibly come from this?" When tough questions like these arise, we can take consolation in a powerful truth repeated all through the Bible: *The Lord is good.*

God is gracious, merciful, and compassionate. He has confirmed this again and again by His past goodness to us. When the psalmist was deeply troubled, he asked, "Has God forgotten to be gracious?" He then answered his own question by saying, "I will remember the works of the LORD; surely I will remember your wonders of old" (77:9,11).

Need encouragement? First, look back. Fill your mind with thoughts of God's goodness to you in the past. Then look ahead...and rest assured in the truth that His goodness will continue into the future.

Hope

Hope can see heaven through the thickest clouds.

THOMAS BROOKS

Growing More like Christ

We know that when He is revealed, we shall be like Him, for we shall see Him as He is.

1 JOHN 3:2

∽

While we Christians are here on earth, we will never resolve "the great tension": We are forgiven and cleansed children of God, and yet we still struggle with and succumb to sin. From a *positional* standpoint, God has declared us fully righteous, but from a *practical* standpoint, we still exhibit from time to time the unrighteous ways of man. The tension between our position and our practice won't disappear until our mortal bodies are changed to immortal ones.

In the meantime, the Holy Spirit is shaping us to become more like Christ. Sometimes this "sculpting" process is slow and painful. We become impatient, wishing for results more quickly. But we read that one day "we *shall* be like Him," and "He who has begun a good work in you *will* complete it" (Philippians 1:6).

When you arrive on heaven's shore, both your position and practice will match perfectly. And that's a harmony you will know *forever*.

Forging Good from Bad

We know that all things work together for good to those who love God.

ROMANS 8:28

∾

Romans 8:28 is perhaps one of the most oft-quoted verses in the Bible...and one of the more frequently misunderstood.

What it's not saying: It's not saying *all* things are good. It's not saying that bad things will somehow *become* good. And it's not saying our lives will be free of trouble, always filled with good.

What it is saying: God has the power to somehow, in ways we don't understand, take the challenges, the difficulties, and the pains of life and forge beautiful results from them. These results can include greater patience, stronger faith, deeper trust, purer motives, truer humility, nobler desires, and a more God-centered life.

Bad will still happen. But somewhere, somehow, good can come from it. That's God's promise to those who love Him.

Lift Up Your Eyes

I will lift up my eyes to the hills—from whence comes my help? My help comes from the LORD, who made heaven and earth.

PSALM 121:1-2

∾

When troubles come, Satan wants us to look downward and inward. He wants us to keep our eyes on our problems, our worries, our sorrows. He wants us to try to climb out of the slippery pit of despair using our own feeble resources.

True help, however, comes only from above. When we need strength, we should seek out someone who is stronger than we are. The answer, then, is to look upward and outward—to look beyond our feeble selves to the Almighty Creator of heaven and earth. He has put His power at our disposal!

And when you lift up your eyes, you'll find your heart lifted up as well—with the hope and comfort that comes from knowing that no crisis is too great for God to handle.

A Savior You Can Count On

Jesus Christ is the same yesterday, today, and forever.

HEBREWS 13:8

∽

If you can count on anyone, Jesus Christ is the One. Because He is perfect, He does not need to change. And because He is faithful, He will not change.

Consider what this means to you: He will never change His mind about your salvation. Retract the forgiveness extended to you. Alter the requirements for getting to heaven. Void any of His promises to you. Negate the spiritual inheritance awaiting you in eternity. Withdraw His presence from you. Diminish in His ability to preserve you, provide for you, and protect you.

In a world full of people and circumstances that change from one moment to the next, the truth that Jesus is always the same is a wonderful source of security. While the winds of change swirl all around us, we can stand firm in the fact that Jesus is the same yesterday, today, and forever.

The Power of Belief

Why are you cast down, O my soul? And why are you disquieted within me? Hope in God.

PSALM 43:5

❧

The ride on the train of discouragement, disappointment, and depression always descends a steep slope. How can we put on the brakes and stop this descent? The psalmist tells us the solution is to "hope in God."

The Puritan writer Richard Sibbes said that "the nature of hope is to expect that which faith believes." Do you believe God is powerful enough to change your circumstances? Do you believe He can use the negative situations of life to bring about positive results in you? Do you believe He loves you so much that even when hope seems to have died, deliverance *will* come?

When the darkness surrounds you, remember what God can do. Don't give up, for no storm lasts forever. Eventually the clouds will clear, and the sun will shine.

Do you believe? If you do, faith will give birth to hope...and turn your descent around into an ascent marked by confidence, peace, and joy.

Faithfulness

When we trustfully resign ourselves,
and all our affairs into God's hands,
fully persuaded of His love and faithfulness,
the sooner shall we be satisfied
with His providence and realize that
"He doeth all things well."

A.W. PINK

A Guaranteed Protection

The LORD is faithful, and he will strengthen and protect you from the evil one.

2 THESSALONIANS 3:3 (NIV)

∽

One characteristic that truly sets God apart from people is that He is *faithful*. What He says, He will do—without hesitation, equivocation, or compromise. Neither the passage of time, nor changes in circumstances, nor those who oppose Him with all their might can undermine the certainty that the Lord will follow through.

God is faithful to keep His promises (Deuteronomy 7:9), to carry our salvation to completion (1 Thessalonians 5:24), to provide a way of escape from temptation (1 Corinthians 10:13), and as the verse at the top of this page says, to strengthen and protect us from Satan.

This means we have no reason to fear our greatest adversary. God *is* faithful; He *will* protect us. What a wonderful assurance! Yet we must still do our part—which is to "submit to God. Resist the devil" (James 4:7).

His Pledge to You

He who calls you is faithful, who also will do it.

1 THESSALONIANS 5:24

∽

In the verse above, what has God promised to be faithful to do? The previous verse gives us the answer: "May the God of peace Himself sanctify you completely; and may your whole spirit, soul, and body be preserved blameless at the coming of our Lord Jesus Christ."

So God not only gives salvation to us as a free gift but also works within us to make us pure. He doesn't say, "Okay, I've saved you from sin. Now it's up to you to stay holy." As 2 Peter 1:3 says, "His divine power has given to us all things that pertain to life and godliness." God doesn't stop at commanding us to obey Him; He gives us the resources that enable us to do what He asks.

And why does God do this? Because He is faithful. He has made a pledge to preserve us till Jesus returns, and He will keep it. Aren't you glad you don't have to count on your own faithfulness?

Sufficiency

You may never know that Jesus is all you need,
until Jesus is all you have.

CORRIE TEN BOOM

All Sufficiency in All Things

God loves a cheerful giver. And God is able to make all grace abound toward you, that you, always having all sufficiency in all things, may have an abundance for every good work.

2 CORINTHIANS 9:7-8

∽

In the manner that you give to others, God will give to you. As you give generously and with discernment to those who have need, God will replenish your supply so that you yourself are never in need. He is "able to make *all* grace abound"—that is, His grace is infinite...so that you will have "*all* sufficiency in *all* things." The repeated use of the qualifier "all" should forever settle in our minds that we will never lack what we truly need.

So ask God to bring to your attention those who have need...and as He does, give generously, knowing that through your actions, you will give others a glimpse of God's abounding goodness. Give cheerfully to others...and God's grace will overflow to you!

Every Good Gift

My God shall supply all your need according to His riches in glory by Christ Jesus.

PHILIPPIANS 4:19

❧

God knows our needs before we ask Him. But sometimes we insist on being self-sufficient and fulfilling our needs in our own power, forgetting or even refusing to go to the Lord and ask. Not until we ask does He bless—James 4:2 says, "You do not have because you do not ask." God desires for us to acknowledge our dependence on Him and recognize Him as the sole source of "every good gift and every perfect gift" (James 1:17).

And when God gives, He does so "according to His riches." He provides for us not merely in a token manner but in proportion to His infinite abundance. The result? Our true needs are fully met. He does this because He cares for us, loves us, delights in us, and promises to be faithful to us.

Total Dependence

Not that we are sufficient of ourselves to think of anything as being from ourselves, but our sufficiency is from God.

2 CORINTHIANS 3:5

∽

Do you realize you can never be too dependent upon God? In fact, He desires that you be fully dependent upon Him—that you ask for His wisdom, strength, and provision in even the smallest details of your life.

The world we live in teaches us to be self-sufficient—to pull up our own bootstraps, to face up to life's challenges, to not buckle under when the going gets tough. We've been so conditioned by this kind of thinking that we hesitate to make our needs known to our brothers and sisters in Christ, and even to God Himself.

You bring God great pleasure when you place your responsibilities, your decisions, your dreams, your family, your possessions—everything great and small—at His feet, asking Him to guide your every step in every matter. The more you depend upon Him, the more He is able to bless you!

Letting God's Power Shine

I can do all things through Christ who strengthens me.

PHILIPPIANS 4:13

∽

Without God's power, Gideon's army of 300 would never have defeated an enemy of 10,000. When David slew Goliath, he placed his confidence in God, not a suit of armor. And as long as Peter looked to Christ, he was able to walk on water. But the moment he glanced downward, he sank.

All through the Bible, we see this important truth again and again: Without God's help, we are nothing. But when we depend wholly on Him...watch out!

Regardless of the difficulty of the circumstance, God will enable you to rise to the occasion. You may experience great pain or heartache. You may struggle with uncertainty or discouragement. Yet such is beneficial, for in our trials, God's power has the opportunity to shine all the more. Do not worry, for God will never fail you.

A Sufficient Grace

*My grace is sufficient for you, for My strength is
made perfect in weakness.*

2 CORINTHIANS 12:9

❧

Can you imagine God turning down a prayer
request from one of the greatest leaders in the New
Testament, the apostle Paul? A request made not once,
not twice, but three times? Paul doesn't tell us what
bothered him. But it must have been serious, for he
"pleaded with the Lord three times." And God's
response? "No...My grace is sufficient for you."

God knew He could accomplish more by showing
His power through Paul's weakness than by removing
Paul's weakness altogether. Is that how you view the
hardships in your life? Have you considered that you
might actually receive greater benefit by persevering
through your weaknesses than by not having them at all?

Without our afflictions, we would not be intimately
acquainted with God's grace and strength. In this sense
we can truly be thankful for our trials...for each one is
yet another opportunity for our all-sufficient God to
display His strength in us and through us.

Every Spiritual Blessing

Blessed be the God and Father of our Lord Jesus Christ, who has blessed us with every spiritual blessing in the heavenly places in Christ.

EPHESIANS 1:3

∽

God has blessed us "with *every* spiritual blessing." In other words, total blessing. Nothing is missing. If you find that hard to believe or imagine, then notice the all-encompassing words the Bible uses elsewhere when referring to God's gifts to us:

- "His divine power has given to us *all* things that pertain to life and godliness" (2 Peter 1:3).

- "You are *complete* in Him, who is the head of all principality and power" (Colossians 2:10).

- "*Every* good gift and *every* perfect gift is from above and comes down from the Father of lights" (James 1:17).

All. Complete. Every. What more could we want? If we feel we're lacking, maybe we've forgotten some (or many!) of our blessings.

He Is Faithful

*Do not worry, saying, "What shall we eat?" or "What
shall we drink?" or "What shall we wear?"...For your
heavenly Father knows that you need all these things.
But seek first the kingdom of God and His righteousness, and all these things shall be added to you.*

MATTHEW 6:31-33

൷

Did you know worry and faith are inconsistent?
Worry says, in effect, "God, I doubt Your ability to meet
my needs." Faith, by contrast, says, "Father, I don't
know *how* You will meet my need, but I know You *will*."

Here in Matthew 6:31-33, Jesus, the Master Physician, prescribes to us the cure for worry. He tells us to
exchange all our earthly distractions for one simple
preoccupation: seeking God's kingdom and being right
with Him. You mind His business, and He will mind
yours.

God's track record speaks for itself. Can we name
any of His own whom the Lord has failed to care for?
Surely the One who has given us every spiritual
blessing in heaven can take care of our every need here
on earth.

He Is Faithful

Fulfillment

The LORD is my shepherd; I shall not want.

PSALM 23:1

Better than a Blank Check

*Delight yourself also in the LORD, and He shall give
you the desires of your heart.*

PSALM 37:4

∽

At first glance, this may appear to be a blank check
to ask God to give you whatever you want. But it isn't.
It's actually better than that. It's an encouragement for
you to delight in Him—for your greatest joy to be
drawing near to Him and loving Him. And when you
do that, you'll find your thoughts, your concerns, and
your heart lining up with His. That which is important
to God will become important to you.

Drawing near to God will have a profound impact
on your desires. God will *want* to fulfill the longings of
your heart because they are His longings, too. And
you'll be much happier because your yearnings will be
for the more noble, more worthy things in life. You'll
be living on a much higher plane, seeking those things
that have eternal value.

Delight in the Lord...and you won't be disap-
pointed!

No Good Gift Spared

He who did not spare His own Son, but delivered Him up for us all, how shall He not with Him also freely give us all things?

ROMANS 8:32

∽

We could call this the promise of all promises. Here is another way to word it: What can God deny us after having given us Jesus? When God gave us His Son, He gave the greatest gift He could possibly give. In light of that, why would God withhold any lesser gifts from us?

The fact is, He won't. And when He gives, He does so freely. We don't need to force His hand. So if you have a genuine need and bring it before the Lord in prayer, you can be assured He will meet it.

"But I have needs that He hasn't met yet," you say. Consider these possibilities: Does God view your *want* as a true *need*? Might He have delayed His answer till a more appropriate time?

When a "need" goes unmet, may your response be one of trusting God's wisdom rather than doubting His goodness.

Exceedingly Abundantly

*Now to Him who is able to do exceedingly abun-
dantly above all that we ask or think, according to
the power that works in us, to Him be glory.*

EPHESIANS 3:20-21

∽

He is able! As Christians, we have a power at work
within us that can do what we cannot. This wonderful
power is manifest in numerous ways:

God has taken us from spiritual death to spiritual
life. The old man is gone, the new man has come. The
fallen has become the resurrected. That which is mortal
will become immortal. We are being transformed into
the image of Christ. We can now say no to sin and yes
to righteousness. We who were once enemies with God
are now His children. As new creatures, we have new
hearts and minds. We are no longer blind, but have the
Holy Spirit within, enabling us to see clearly and truly
understand God's Word.

And He does so much more for us! Yes, He is able.
His power is unlimited. May we never take His work
in us for granted or fail to thank Him.

Sharing His Riches

The Spirit Himself bears witness with our spirit that we are children of God...and joint heirs with Christ.

ROMANS 8:16-17

&

Everything that exists in this universe belongs to Christ by divine right. Hebrews 1:2 tells us that God's Son has been "appointed heir of all things." By no means is this limited to the things of this earth; all that is in heaven and the spiritual realm belongs to Him, too.

And because of Christ's work on the cross, in which He took on our unrighteousness and gave us His righteousness, *we are joint heirs with Christ!* That which belongs to Him belongs to us, too. Earthly kings rarely share their wealth with their subjects. By contrast, Christ desires to share all that belongs to Him. We will partake in His honor and riches. We will rule alongside Him, and we will share in His glory.

Second Corinthians 2:8-9 puts it all into perspective for us: "Christ...though He was rich, yet for your sakes He became poor, that you through His poverty might become rich." Have you thanked Him?

Protection

One Almighty is more than all mighties.

WILLIAM GURNALL

Your Great Advocate

If God is for us, who can be against us?

ROMANS 8:31

∽

God guards and protects those who belong to Him. Now, that doesn't mean the path of life will always be smooth. We will encounter people who oppose us and are determined to harm us. Satan will never grow tired of luring us into sin. And notice that James said, "Count it all joy *when* you fall into various trials," not "*if* you fall into various trials." So difficulties and enemies are a certainty for us.

But in the midst of the tough times and persecution, "God is for us." He is our shield, our security, our Protector. God's power to give us victory is greater than any power that might attempt to defeat us. He can overrule all things, and nothing can overrule Him.

God is on your side. He's the greatest advocate you could ever have fighting for you!

A Very Present Help

God is our refuge and strength, a very present help in trouble.

PSALM 46:1

↬

The words of Psalm 46 inspired Martin Luther to write the majestic song "A Mighty Fortress Is Our God." A fortress is appropriate imagery because it portrays the fact that God is both our refuge *and* our strength. He provides for us a protective shelter that cannot be penetrated even in the fiercest of battles, and at the same time, He equips and empowers us so we can have strategic advantage over our foes.

God is also a "*very* present help" in trouble. He is even closer to us than the trouble itself. His availability to us is instant. With Him, help is never "on the way," it's already with us.

As Martin Luther said, "Though this world with devils filled should threaten to undo us, we will not fear, for God hath willed His truth to triumph through us."

Comfort

*The better we understand God's Word,
the more comfort we can find in it;
the darkness of trouble arises from
the darkness of ignorance.*

MATTHEW HENRY

The Wisdom of Waiting on God

I waited patiently for the LORD; and He inclined to me, and heard my cry.

PSALM 40:1

∽

Have you ever wished God would hurry up? Sometimes, in our eagerness for results, we run ahead of Him and attempt to make things happen in our own power, without His help. And in the end, the results are never as good as they would have been if we had just waited for God.

Patience is a difficult discipline to cultivate. But it has many benefits. It helps us to check with God first. To wait on His timing. To carefully consider all the alternatives. And to have His divine power at our disposal instead of mere human strength.

Even Jesus waited on God. Early in the morning, He sought God in prayer, waiting for direction and blessing. He had come to do His Father's will, and He paused to make sure He knew what it was before taking action.

Wait...and God will answer.

His Incomparable Care

*Humble yourselves...casting all your care upon Him,
for He cares for you.*

1 PETER 5:6-7

∽

Are you staggering under a weight that your Father in heaven is more than capable of carrying for you? Do you doubt His earnest willingness to help you with the burden that preoccupies you now? Once again, we find within a promise the liberating word "all"! We're to turn *every* concern over to God, regardless of how small it is. The word "casting" means "flinging away"—we are literally commanded to throw our distracting anxieties off our frail shoulders and into His omnipotent hands.

God never intended for us to wear ourselves out over worries. He wants to free us of distractions so we can focus our energies on those things that build up, not weigh down. Repeatedly in the Scriptures, He tells us to rest in Him and not fret.

Resign your problem to Him. *Rest* in His calming grace. And let Him *renew* you by His refreshing power. Give your cares to your Father...and let Him do what only He can do!

He Loves the Unlovely

He heals the brokenhearted and binds up their wounds.

PSALM 147:3

∽

We live in a world that adores the rich and the beautiful, and exalts the strong and the powerful. This has been a problem even within the church—the apostle James had to chastise some believers who were showing favoritism to the rich and disregard for the poor (James 2:1-9).

Yet our high and mighty God chooses to lower Himself and walk among the weak and the wounded. He loves the unlovely and sympathizes with the sick. Few people are willing to spare the time to comfort those whose lives are broken...but God takes special delight in nursing them back to health.

When your life has fallen apart and others have forgotten or abandoned you, your heavenly Father will remain at your side. You will never exhaust His compassions, for they are new every morning. Great is His faithfulness!

The Master Comforter

Praise be to the God and Father of our Lord Jesus Christ, the Father of compassion and the God of all comfort, who comforts us in all our troubles, so that we can comfort those in any trouble with the comfort we ourselves have received from God.

2 CORINTHIANS 1:3-4 (NIV)

&

Suffering not only drives us closer to God but also equips us to become messengers of comfort and encouragement to others.

If *anyone* can console us, He can...because only He can see clearly into our hearts and minds and understand our need perfectly.

And after we experience His healing touch, we can take what we've learned and pass it along to others who are faced with similar challenges. Such comfort is powerful because we're revealing to others what we learned from the Master Comforter Himself.

So even if you never come to understand why God allowed a certain trial in your life, you're still assured of two unquestionably significant benefits: God will comfort you, and you will then be able to comfort others.

The Promise of a Great Future

*God will wipe away every tear from their eyes; there
shall be no more death, nor sorrow, nor crying. There
shall be no more pain, for the former things have
passed away.*

REVELATION 21:4

∽

Pain and sorrow are so intertwined into the every-
day fabric of our lives that we can't imagine what the
world would be like without them. But consider the
results of pain: Anxiety. Discouragement. Depression.
Grief. Hurt. Bondage. Division. Anger. Bitterness. Empti-
ness. Loss. Darkness. Defeat.

Yet a day is coming when these will pass away, and
we will never experience them again. Instead, we will
know the very best of all God has to offer: Peace. Hope.
Happiness. Joy. Comfort. Freedom. Unity. Love. Sweet-
ness. Fullness. Gain. Light. Victory. And so much more!

The tears we shed—whether from our eyes or in
our heart—will one day be gone, never to come back.
God Himself will wipe them away and usher us into
the new heaven and new earth, into a paradise where
we will never again know sorrow.

Confidence

Assurance...enables a child of God to feel that
the great business of life is a settled business,
the great debt a paid debt,
the great disease a healed disease
and the great work a finished work.

J.C. RYLE

A Perfect Track Record

[Abraham] did not waver at the promise of God through unbelief, but was strengthened in faith, giving glory to God, and being fully convinced that what He had promised He was also able to perform.

ROMANS 4:20-21

✏

Even when Abraham was 100 years old and Sarah was 90, Abraham was convinced God would keep His promise that he would have a son and become the father of many nations.

Noah was convinced God would send a worldwide flood and spent 120 years building an ark. Moses was convinced God would set His people free, and he challenged the Pharaoh and all of Egypt.

All through the Bible and across many centuries stretches a long line of saints who were convinced God would keep His promises. And in every instance, God followed through. Not once can we point to a broken promise.

Are you convinced? Or do you waver in unbelief? That which God promises, He *will* perform. His track record is perfect. Rest in His promises...and believe!

God Is Able

*My counsel shall stand, and I will do all My
pleasure....Indeed I have spoken it; I will also bring
it to pass. I have purposed it; I will also do it.*

ISAIAH 46:10-11

℘

We can never exhaust the reservoir of God's power
or empty the ocean of His strength. Whatever work
God begins, He is able to sustain and to complete.
Whatever plans He makes, He is able to carry out and
achieve. Whatever purpose He establishes, He is able
to maintain and accomplish. And whatever promise He
utters, He is able to act on and fulfill.

Are you anxious about finding the strength to make
it through today? Are you unable to figure out why
God has allowed certain things to happen? Are you
tempted to question God's purpose? Are you waiting as
a promise seems to go unkept?

Remember...God's counsel will stand. Whatever He
decides will happen. He will keep you in His plan and
purpose, and He will keep His promises. Of this you
can be sure: He will never fail you.

Righteousness Will Prevail

*Do not fret because of evildoers, nor be envious of
the workers of iniquity. For they shall soon be cut
down like the grass, and wither as the green herb.*

PSALM 37:1

&

The Bible repeatedly assures us that God punishes
the wicked and rewards the righteous. But sometimes
we find this hard to believe. Justice is not always
served. The wicked prosper while the righteous suffer.
Why is this so?

We live in a world that chose to reject God's rulership, and because of the Lord's great mercy, He has not
yet taken that rulership back. As He allows evil to run
its course, His desire is that people will see the futility
of their ways and turn to Him. In the meantime, Psalm
37:1 tells us, "Do not fret."

Then we're told the cure for a fretful heart: "Trust
in the LORD, and do good" (verse 3). We're to let God
handle those who do evil while we focus on doing
good.

Someday, righteousness *will* prevail. And when it
does, it will do so for eternity.

Always Providing

I have been young, and now am old; yet I have not seen the righteous forsaken, nor his descendants begging for bread.

PSALM 37:25

෴

One of the Old Testament names for God is Jehovah-Jireh, or "The Lord Will Provide." Taking care of our needs is literally a part of who He is.

Unfortunately, we tend to think of our Father as our provider only in our times of need. For every day that we wonder where our next dollar will come from, we enjoy many days when a dollar is already in hand. For every occasion an unexpected crisis occurs, we see many occasions when all goes smoothly as planned. For every time a circumstance forces us to our knees in prayer, we glide through other times when we don't pray because we see no reason to.

Yet God's providence is as much at work in the less needy times as in the needy. As James 1:17 says, "*Every good gift and every perfect gift is from above.*" The more we make an effort to consciously thank God for *everything* at *all* times, the more we will be able to see just how much He really does provide for us.

Answered Prayer

Never was a faithful prayer lost.
Some prayers have a longer voyage than others,
but then they return with their richer lading at last,
so that the praying soul is a gainer by waiting for an answer.

WILLIAM GURNALL

He Hears Your Prayers

This is the confidence that we have in Him, that if we ask anything according to His will, He hears us.

1 JOHN 5:14

❧

Embracing the will of God is the highest attainment of prayer. If the petitions we lift up to our heavenly Father are in harmony with His purposes, we can be *fully confident* He will hear them. Of course, He might not answer in the manner or the time that we expect, for He knows the need better than we do, and He will orchestrate His reply to conform to His higher and nobler design for our lives.

How can we ensure that our prayers are "according to His will"?

Keep in mind that we pray not to *inform* God's mind, for He already knows all things even before we ask. We pray not to *change* His mind, for He already has a plan in place and knows what is best. Rather, we pray to *receive* His mind—to ask Him to place His desires in our hearts so we can become cooperative instruments of the work He desires to do on the earth.

Whatever You Ask

I say to you, whatever things you ask when you pray, believe that you receive them, and you will have them.

MARK 11:24

❧

This seems a very bold statement from Jesus. Does He literally mean that *whatever* we pray for, we *will* receive? Anything at all?

First John 5:14 helps complete the picture for us: "This is the confidence that we have in Him, that if we ask anything *according to His will,* He hears us." So we are free to bring our every request...but we must also realize God always works according to His perfect will and according to what He knows is best for us. If He grants our request, He does so because it conforms with His higher plan and purpose. And when He does not, His higher love knows what is really better for us.

God would much rather we expand our prayer requests to Him, allowing Him to teach us through His yes and no answers, than limit our petitions because we are unsure of how He might answer. In this way, you will learn to trust His wisdom.

Blessings Are His Pleasure

*Ask, and it will be given to you; seek, and you will
find; knock, and it will be opened to you. For every-
one who asks receives, and he who seeks finds, and
to him who knocks it will be opened.*

MATTHEW 7:7-8

❧

Verse 11 sheds even more light on the words above:
"If you then, being evil, know how to give good gifts
to your children, how much more will your Father
who is in heaven give good things to those who ask
Him!" In the same way that human parents know their
children's needs better than children do, our Father in
heaven knows our needs better than we do.

Our Father's storehouse in heaven abounds with
blessings for us, and He takes great pleasure in pouring
out those blessings on us. That's why He tells us to ask,
to seek, to knock. He *wants* our petitions! Yet too often
our requests are earthly minded. Or we place con-
straints on God, telling Him how we expect Him to
respond. Instead of limiting Him, or asking amiss, why
not give Him a blank check and let Him answer
according to His infinite wisdom and grace?

Becoming Mighty in Prayer

If you abide in Me, and My words abide in you, you
will ask what you desire, and it shall be done for you.

JOHN 15:7

❧

The key to answered prayer rests on a very big
"if"—if you abide in Christ and let His Word abide in
you. This abiding means becoming so intimately joined
to the Lord that His wishes become yours. As the great
English minister C.H. Spurgeon said, "The *carte blanche*
can only be given to one whose very life is, 'Not I, but
Christ liveth in me.'"

If you wish to be mighty in prayer, Christ must be
mighty in you. Jesus confirms this two verses earlier,
where He said, "He who abides in Me, and I in him,
bears much fruit; for without Me you can do nothing"
(verse 5).

Are you abiding in Him? Your honest answer will
determine the difference between powerless pleading
and powerful praying.

A God Who Hears

The LORD has heard my cry for mercy; the LORD accepts my prayer.

PSALM 6:9 (NIV)

✑

God is a Shepherd who listens with a ready ear for the cries of His sheep. He is ever alert to our pleas for help. He invites us to come before Him with our needs. He is never unavailable or unconcerned. He's eager to care for us, and we need only to remember to come into His presence.

We often try to take life by the horns ourselves. Somehow being tough and self-sufficient seems more virtuous. But we need to remember that our Father's wisdom and strength are infinitely greater than our own and that we have much to gain by seeking His help in every circumstance. May we never hesitate to cry out to Him; may we live in constant readiness to seek Him in prayer...because He *will* listen, and He *will* accept our prayer.

Success

God's definition of success:

*"Let not the wise man glory in his wisdom,
let not the mighty man glory in his might,
nor let the rich man glory in his riches;
but let him who glories glory in this,
that he understands and knows Me, that I am the* LORD,
*exercising lovingkindness, judgment, and righteousness in the
earth. For in these I delight," says the* LORD.

JEREMIAH 9:23-24

The Key to Success

*This Book of the Law shall not depart from your
mouth, but you shall meditate in it day and night,
that you may observe to do according to all that is
written in it. For then you will make your way pros-
perous, And then you will have good success.*

JOSHUA 1:8

∽

What is the connection between applying God's
Word to your life and knowing success?

The Bible is like an instruction manual for a tech-
nologically complex gadget. When you follow the
instructions for usage, the device won't break down or
malfunction. And when you adhere to the Bible—the
instruction manual for human living—the same is true.
As complicated as life is, we need all the help we can
get! As A.W. Pink says, "We cannot expect the God of
Truth to be with us if we neglect the Truth of God."

Notice that according to Joshua 1:8, merely reading
or knowing the Bible is not enough. We are "to do
according to all that is written in it." Only then can it
make a difference *in* us and *through* us and *for* us. Only
then will we know success as God defines it.

Leaning on God

Trust in the LORD with all your heart, and lean not on your own understanding; in all your ways acknowledge Him, and He shall direct your paths.

PROVERBS 3:5-6

❧

Are you looking for clearer direction in a specific matter? Are you having trouble making a decision? Are you worried about the future? Proverbs 3:5-6 offers good counsel:

Trust Him with all your heart: Do only what you can do, and then leave the results to God. Don't be anxious; trust in the Lord. Worry cannot do anything, but God can do everything.

Lean not on your own understanding: If you can't figure it out, don't try to. Remember, God can see everything, including the future. Lean on *His* understanding.

In all your ways acknowledge Him: That's *all* your ways. Let Him have complete control. Put Him first. Recognize what He can do and has already done.

And He shall direct your paths: When you are fully trusting, fully yielding, and fully honoring God, He can then fully direct your paths.

286

His Devotion to Us

Because he has set his love upon Me, therefore I will deliver him; I will set him on high, because he has known My name.

PSALM 91:14

❦

Here, God describes the blessings He gives to those who have set their love on Him and know His name. Once again we see the great lengths to which God is eager to shower His grace on us. Our devotion to Him stirs His devotion to us. And what a devotion it is! He promises to deliver us and to set us "on high."

To be set "on high" means to be exalted. How? This can happen as we receive a number of things: a position of honor, a role as a leader, a responsibility as a role model, a stewardship over significant resources, great usefulness or success, special insight or wisdom, or triumph over temptation.

The priority, of course, is our affection for God. Let us not pursue the blessings themselves, but the Lord alone. Then the blessings will come!

Notes

1. A.W. Tozer, *The Knowledge of the Holy* (San Francisco: Harper & Row, 1961), p. 116.

2. A.W. Pink, *Gleanings in the Godhead* (Chicago: Moody Press, 1975), p. 47.

3. Stephen Charnock, *The Existence and Attributes of God*, vol. 2 (Grand Rapids: Baker Book House, 1996), p. 211.

4. John MacArthur, *The Love of God*, (Dallas: Word Publishing, 1969), p. 169.

5. Christopher Christian Sturm, *Morning Communings with God*, vol. 1 (London: Baldwin, Cradock, and Joy, 1825), p. 49.

6. A.W. Tozer, *The Knowledge of the Holy* (San Francisco: Harper & Row, 1961), p. 62.

7. Dinsdale Young, *C.H. Spurgeon's Prayers* (London: Passmore & Alabaster, 1905), p. 148.

8. Thomas Watson, *Puritan Sermons,* vol. 2 (Wheaton, IL: Richard Owen Roberts Publishing, 1981), pp. 62-64.